SPECTRUM

Writing

Grade 5

SPECTRUM

Columbus, Ohio

Credits:

School Specialty Publishing Editorial/Art & Design Team
Vincent F. Douglas, *President*
Tracey E. Dils, *Publisher*
Jennifer Blashkiw Pawley, *Project Editor*
Suzanne M. Diehm, *Project Editor*
Rose Audette, *Art Director*

Contributors:
Duncan Searl
Claire Norman
Dr. Betty Jane Wagner
Jan Kennedy
Virginia Allison

Also Thanks to:
Illustrated Alaskan Moose Inc., *Cover Illustration*
4ward Communications, *Interior Design and Production*
Jenny Campbell, *Interior Illustration*

Send all inquiries to:
School Specialty Publishing
8720 Orion Place
Columbus, OH 43240-2111

ISBN 1-57768-915-1

8 9 10 11 12 13 POH 11 10 09 08 07 06

Table of Contents

Table of Contents

Things to Remember About Writing

Prewriting

- Brainstorm topics you might like to write about.
- Create a list of things you could write about each topic.
- Choose the topic you know the most about and that would be of interest to others.
- Collect information.

Writing

- Use sentences in a paragraph only if they tell about the main idea of the paragraph.
- Write directions for doing something in proper order.
- Remember to use sequence words like *first*, *next*, and *last* to put events in the proper order.
- Use *er* or *est*, *more* or *most* to compare things.
- Use details to tell how something looks, sounds, smells, tastes, or feels.
- Think about your purpose before you start writing.
- Write a rough draft focusing on what you want to say rather than the spelling, punctuation, and grammar. You will have the opportunity to make corrections later.

Revising

- Read your rough draft, making changes for interest and clarity.
- Use words that are exact to make your sentences clear.
- Be sure every sentence has a subject and a verb.
- Combine sentences to make your writing smoother.
- Make all verbs in a paragraph or story tell about the same time (verb tense).
- Ask a parent or friend to read your writing and offer suggestions for improvement.

Proofreading

Check to see that:
- you used capital letters correctly.
- you put in correct punctuation marks.
- you used proper grammar.
- all words are spelled correctly.
- you used correct verb forms.

Proofreading Checklist

Use this checklist when proofreading your writing. It will help you remember things you may forget as you review your work.

☐ Does each sentence being with a capital letter and end with a period, question mark, or exclamation point?
☐ Does each sentence have a subject and verb and a complete thought?
☐ Are there any fragments or run-on sentences?
☐ Are all words capitalized that should be?
☐ Are all words spelled correctly?
☐ Have you used troublesome verbs? If so, have you used the correct forms?
☐ Does each subject agree with its verb?
☐ Did you choose exact words to make your writing clear?
☐ Does each pronoun agree with the word it refers to?
☐ Have you used apostrophes correctly - to show contractions or possessives?
☐ Have all necessary commas been correctly inserted?
☐ Have you checked the grammar and usage in your writing?
☐ Have you indented your paragraphs?

Proofreading Marks

Use these proofreading marks to help you make corrections in your writing. Try to use a colored pencil or pen when you proofread so that your marks will stand out.

≡	capital letter	Max smith
/	lowercase letter	We like to Eat…
⊙	add period	It was fun⊙
?	add question mark	Do you like pizza?
∧	insert, add this	Ten people were coming…
✃	delete, take out	Jump all around
∨	add apostrophe	The bike was Sarahs.
¶	new paragraph	happy.¶The boy…
∾	transpose, switch the order	the child so toy
∧	add a comma	hiking, biking fishing
⬭	check spelling	I didn't beleive her.

Capitalization
Sentences, People, Pets

- The first word in a sentence is capitalized.
  My best friend is named Marco.

- The names of people and pets are capitalized. Titles of respect such as **Miss**, **Mr.**, **Mrs.**, **Ms.**, and **Dr.** are capitalized. Do not capitalize doctor unless it is part of a name.
  Yesterday **M**arco let me walk **F**reckles, his new puppy.
  Freckles's veterinarian is **D**r. Williamson. He is a kind **d**octor.

- The pronoun **I** is capitalized.
  I've always wanted a puppy.

- The title of a relative is capitalized only if it is used as a name or part of a name.
  Marco's **f**ather offered to give me a puppy.
  I asked **M**other if I could have one.
  She said **F**ather and **U**ncle **J**ack are both allergic to dogs.

Practice

Read the paragraph below. Circle the five words that should begin with a capital letter. Draw a line through two letters that are capitalized and should not be.

> I wish you could meet aunt Rita. She's not really my Aunt, but since she's such a good friend of Mom's, I've always called her that. Aunt Rita works at a bakery, and whenever she visits, she brings me something different. that's not the only reason i like her. Aunt Rita is one of those people who makes you feel really important. when I told her I wanted to be a Doctor, she took me seriously. I'm pretty lucky to have a friend like Aunt rita.

Capitalization
Places, Holidays, Events

- The names of days, months, and holidays are capitalized. The names of the seasons are not capitalized.
    This summer, my father took me on a vacation. We left on a **T**uesday in **M**ay, right after **M**emorial **D**ay.

- Direction words are capitalized only when they name a region.
    We drove south from our home in the **N**ortheast.

- The names of places, buildings, and monuments are capitalized.
    In **W**ashington, **D.C.**, we saw the **L**incoln **M**emorial and the **W**hite **H**ouse.

- Important events are capitalized. Always capitalize the names of legislative bodies, such as the Congress, Senate, and House of Representatives.
    We also visited the memorial to the **V**ietnam **W**ar.
    The **S**enate was in session during our visit.

Practice

Read the sentences. Circle the ten words that should begin with a capital letter.

1. Mount saint helens is an active volcano.

2. It is part of the cascade range.

3. It is located in the southern part of washington.

4. The volcano erupted on may 18, 1980, killing more than 60 people.

5. In 1982, the national volcano monument was built there.

6. If you ever travel to the northwest, you should try to visit the monument.

Capitalization
Titles of Written Works

- Titles of books, magazines, movies, plays, stories, reports, poems, and songs are capitalized. Always capitalize the first and last word.

  National Geographic

  "Cinderella"

  Johnny Tremain

- Articles (*a*, *an*, *the*) and short conjunctions (*but*, *and*) or prepositions (*of*, *to*) in titles are not capitalized unless they are the first or last words.

  Romeo and Juliet

  "The Battle Hymn of the Republic"

  James and the Giant Peach

Practice

The following titles are all in lowercase letters. Rewrite each title with the proper capitalization. If the title is in italics, underline it when you write it.

1. "every time i climb a tree" _____

2. "who has seen the wind?" _____

3. *brutus the wonder poodle* _____

4. *my buddy, the king* _____

5. *bridge to terabithia* _____

6. *the adventures of tom sawyer* _____

7. "the gettysburg address" _____

8. "puff the magic dragon" _____

Proofreading Practice:
Capitalization

As you read the story below, you will notice that no words have been capitalized. Read the sentences carefully. Use the proofreader's mark (≡) to show which letters should be capitalized.

Christa McAuliffe

christa's interest in the space program began when she was a seventh-grade student and watched alan shephard, the united states' first astronaut, go into space. she was filled with excitement.

christa loved history. when she grew up she became a social studies teacher. when the opportunity arose for school teachers to apply for the next shuttle mission into space, christa was one of over 11,000 teachers who applied. imagine her exhilaration when she was the one chosen.

christa left her teaching position and her family behind in concord, new hampshire to train for her mission. her dream was coming true. she was planning to record every moment to show students that space travel could indeed be a part of their future.

then a terrible thing happened. the shuttle she was on, the *Challenger*, broke apart shortly after liftoff on january 28, 1986. christa and six other crew members lost their lives.

Punctuation
Commas in Series, Introductions, and Direct Address

- A comma is used to separate lists of items in a sentence. Place a comma after each item.
My grandmother sent me to the store for tomatoes, lettuce, cucumbers, and celery.

- Some items on the list might have more than one word. Think of each group of words as an item.
I'm always happy to do chores, run errands, or keep my grandmother company.

- A comma is also used after introductory words such as *yes*, *no*, and *well*.
Well, I had lost the shopping list by the time I got to the store.

- If a speaker addresses someone by name, use a comma to separate the name from the rest of the sentence.
"Thank you for going to the store for me, Tony."
"Grandmother, wait to thank me until you see what I bought."

Practice

In the paragraph below, add eight commas where they are needed.

Endangered species are animals that are in danger of becoming extinct. The cheetah the Asian elephant the snow leopard and the spider monkey are all endangered animals. The animals living in lakes rivers or the ocean are harmed when humans produce water pollution. When land is cleared for houses or other uses, the animals who live there may die. Some animals are endangered because too many have been killed for their fur tusks bones or other products used by people.

Punctuation
Commas with Introductory Phrases and Clauses

- Commas are used to separate an introductory phrase or clause from the rest of a sentence. Introductory phrases start some sentences. They might tell when or where something happened, using words like *after, when, while,* and *before.*

    After the snowfall, we put on our warm clothes and went to the hill behind our school.

    When we got to the school, Tricia and Suzanne were already there.

- Words like *although, if,* and *because* also start some sentences as part of a longer phrase or clause. The comma should follow the end of the phrase or clause.

    Although it was cold, we couldn't wait to start sailing down the hill.

    If you run and jump on your sled, it goes even faster.

    Because the hill was so steep, we kept tumbling off the sled at the bottom.

Practice

Add commas where they are needed in the paragraph below.

When my grandmother was a young girl she decided she wanted to be a doctor. Although almost all doctors were men at that time she didn't let anything stop her. When she talked about her dream nobody thought she was serious. If they had really known her they would have believed her. While she was in college she worked and saved every penny. After she graduated she surprised everyone by going to medical school. Because she was so determined her classmates respected her. Before she graduated she had job offers from many hospitals. If you need a good doctor I would recommend my grandmother.

Proofreading Practice:
Commas

You have learned that commas are used in sentences for several reasons. They are used

1. to separate a series of words or things.
    We had chicken, vegetables, and cake at the banquet.

2. to set off words of direct address.
    Richard, here is your hat.

3. to set off an introductory expression.
    Finally, I passed the test!

4. when two sentences are combined.
    Mary had a soda, and Tom had ice cream.

5. to set off appositives. (A word or phrase that explains a noun preceding it.)
    Fido, our neighbor's dog, takes our paper every morning.

As you read the sentences below, you will notice that commas are missing. Read the sentences carefully. Use the proofreader's mark (∧) to show where commas should be added.

1. Laura Emily Jane and Meghan met at the movies.

2. Sue Ellen the Smith's daughter goes to college in Columbus Ohio.

3. My mom gave me a book and Dad gave me a record.

4. Here take this to the office.

5. We gave Miss Jones our teacher a going away gift.

6. The horse jumped over the fence ran down the road and hid in the barn.

7. Casey likes noodles but he does not like spaghetti.

8. Christopher come help me carry this box.

9. We went to our neighbors the Mays for dinner last night.

10. The team played Monday night Tuesday afternoon and last night.

Possessives
Singular and Plural Forms

If you want to show that something belongs to one person, you add an **-'s**.

- The hairdresser cut **Susan's** hair first.
  Then she styled Mrs. **Harris's** hair.

- If you want to show that something belongs to more than one person, add just an apostrophe (**'**).
  All of the people in the shop know how to cut **kids'** hair.
  The two **hairdressers'** scissors made a snipping sound.

- You can follow the rules above to show that something belongs to a thing, too.
  All of the **shop's** seats were taken.

- Some words are already in the possessive form. You do not have to add anything to them. These words are **my**, **your**, **his**, **her**, **its**, **our**, and **their**. They are called possessive pronouns.
  Roberto got **his** hair cut.
  I decided to get **my** hair cut, too.

Practice

Rewrite each phrase using a possessive. The first one is done for you.

1. the dress that belongs to Katie   _____Katie's dress_____

2. the pet that belongs to all of the students   _____

3. the shoes that belong to Marcus   _____

4. the car that belongs to him   _____

5. the toothbrush that belongs to me   _____

6. the cat that belongs to all of the girls   _____

7. the skates that belong to them   _____

Possessives
Plural vs. Possessive Forms

- You usually add an **-s** or **-es** to make a noun plural.
  I have two excellent **friends**.

- You add **-'s** to show something belongs to someone.
  My friend **Julie's** favorite thing to do is go to movies.

- One mistake some writers make is to add an apostrophe (**'**) when making a word plural. You do not need an apostrophe to make a word plural.
  My other **friend's** favorite thing to do is ride bikes.
  I like to do the things that both my **friends** like to do.

- You use an apostrophe to show that something belongs to someone or something.

Practice

Write the correct word in the blank. If you choose a word with an apostrophe, underline the word that names what belongs to the person or thing you wrote in the blank.

1. The _____ car was very small and painted blue. (clowns, clown's)

2. The _____ all laughed as the clown tumbled out. (kids, kid's)

3. Then three more _____ ran into the circus ring. (clowns, clown's)

4. The _____ eyes grew as the clowns came into the stands. (kids, kids')

5. One clown gave two _____ some pop-up paper flowers. (girls, girl's)

6. Another clown took quarters out of two _____ ears! (boys, boys')

7. A third clown held a ladder for three _____ to climb. (dogs, dogs')

8. The _____ collars were big and ruffled. (dogs, dogs')

9. The fourth clown blew huge _____. (bubbles, bubble's)

10. The _____ applause filled the circus tent. (crowds, crowd's)

Proofreading Practice:
Possessives

As you read the article below, you will notice that apostrophes have not been added to show possessives. Read the sentences carefully. Use the proofreader's mark (⌄) to show where apostrophes need to be added. For extra practice, use the proofreader's mark (≡) to correct errors in capitalization.

Baseball's Beginnings

baseball may have developed from an old english sport of the 1600s called rounders. despite evidence of baseballs connection with rounders, some people believe baseball was invented in 1839 by a man named abner doubleday in cooperstown, new york. in an attempt to settle this argument, a special commission was appointed, and it came to the decision in 1907 that doubleday was indeed the inventor of the modern game.

alexander cartwright was the first to start a baseball club, the knickerbockers. Cartwrights written set of baseball rules made the game much like baseball today. early players received no money to play. in 1869, the cincinnati red stockings became baseballs first team to be paid, making them the first professional baseball team.

Contractions

- A **contraction** is two words written together as one word. One or more letters are taken out of the word to make it shorter. An apostrophe (') shows where the letter or letters are missing.

  it is—**it's**   had not—**hadn't**
  you are—**you're**   has not—**hasn't**
  they are—**they're**   have not—**haven't**
  cannot—**can't**   who is—**who's**
  I will—**I'll**   you will—**you'll**
  I would—**I'd**   could not—**couldn't**

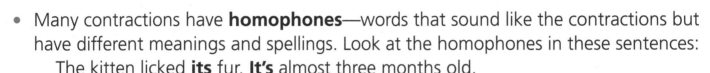

- Sometimes a contraction does more than just take out letters. It changes the letters.
  will not—**won't**

- Many contractions have **homophones**—words that sound like the contractions but have different meanings and spellings. Look at the homophones in these sentences:
  The kitten licked **its** fur. **It's** almost three months old.
  You're lucky to have a kitten. It likes to sleep in **your** bed.

- Contractions are used in informal writing or in stories to show how someone speaks. You probably should not use contractions in a business letter or a formal essay or report.

Practice

Write a contraction for the underlined words in each sentence.

1. I <u>cannot</u> go with you to the movies.   _____

2. My mom <u>will not</u> let me go.   _____

3. She said <u>it is</u> too late to go out.   _____

4. Besides, I <u>have not</u> done my homework yet.   _____

5. Now I wish I <u>had not</u> watched TV after school. _____

Proofreading Practice:
Contractions

As you read the journal entry below, you will notice that
no contractions have been used. Read the sentences carefully.
Write the correct contraction above each underlined word pair.

Space Camp

Blast-off to space camp! <u>I am</u> off to a city in the southwestern United States.
I will be there for a whole month. I <u>could not</u> sleep well last night because I was
so excited.

<u>We will</u> spend the first week in buildings which have chambers that simulate
feelings in space. One of the buildings contains an anti-gravity chamber.

The second week <u>we will</u> sit behind mock control panels to learn what all of
the buttons, dials, and levers do.

During the third week <u>we will</u> each be fitted for a space suit and will learn
how to use all of its features. Then <u>we will</u> be taught how to eat and drink
in space.

Week four will be the most exciting time of all. We step into the space camp
shuttle for the first time and take a mock flight into space. <u>We will</u> use all that
<u>we have</u> learned during the month for our journey to the stars.

Homophones
New/Knew, No/Know,
Here/Hear, Right/Write, There/Their

The following pairs of words are **homophones**. Homophones are words that sound alike but are spelled differently and have different meanings. After you read the definitions, fill in each blank with the correct word.

- **New** means "recently come into existence or the opposite of old."
  Knew is the past tense of the verb know, which means "to be certain of something; be aware of."

    It was the first day of my _____ paper route.

    I _____ it would be a good day.

- **No** means "not so; the opposite of yes." **Know** means "to be certain of something; to be aware of."

    Oh, _____, I thought.

    I _____ I broke Ms. Jackson's window when I threw the newspaper.

- **Here** means "in this place." **Hear** means "to listen to something."

    I couldn't _____ anyone.

    I knocked on the door and said, "Is anybody _____?"

- **Right** means "correct." It can also mean a direction, as in your "right hand."
  Write means "to put down something on paper."

    I decided to _____ a note to Ms. Jackson.

    I knew that would be the _____ thing to do.

- **There** means "in or at that place; to or toward." **Their** is a possessive pronoun "belonging to them."

    I will go _____ and leave a note for the Jacksons.
    I hope they won't be too upset when they find out _____ window is broken.

Proofreading Practice:
Homophones

As you read the journal entry below, you will notice that some of the words have been used incorrectly. Read the sentences carefully, Use the proofreader's mark (⅋) to show which words should be deleted. Write the correct words above them.

The Right Combination

It was the first day at my knew school. I was a little apprehensive. I had all knew supplies in my backpack: spiral notebooks, pens, pencils, ruler, protractor, and calculator. I located my locker on the second floor. Their was a shiny, new combination lock on it. Other kids were opening there lockers and putting jackets and supplies away. It occurred to me that I did not no the combination of my lock. How did they all know theirs? Should I ask, or would they laugh at me? The bell would ring soon. I couldn't be late for class on the first day. As I stood their, kids went by and said hello to me. Then they kept asking me when my birthday was. I thought that was a strange question. Why were they asking about my birthday? Wait a minute! I held the combination lock in my hand and tried the numbers of my birth date 10-28-86. Presto! I found the write number. My locker opened. My day was saved.

Articles

A, **an**, and **the** are articles. They are words that are used before a noun.

- **The** is called a definite article. It is used to let your reader know you are talking about something definite, or specific.
  I went to see **the movie** that everyone is talking about.

- **A** and **an** are indefinite articles. Use them to let your reader know that the noun does not refer to anything or anyone specific.
  I wanted to buy **a snack**, but everything was too expensive!
  Next time I go to **a movie**, I'll eat before I go.

- When the noun you are using begins with a consonant or a vowel that sounds like a consonant, you use **a**. In *one*, *o* sounds like *w*.

a one-story house	**a sidewalk**	**a library**
a book	**a boy**	**a hero**

- When the noun begins with a vowel (a, e, i, o, u) or sounds like it does, you use **an**. In *hour*, the *h* is silent, so you use **an** with it.

an hour	**an octopus**	**an apple**
an owl	**an elephant**	**an honor**

Practice

Underline the correct article in each set of parentheses.

I made (a, the) new friend today. He lives down (a, the) street from me. He
1   2

was riding his bike on (a, the) sidewalk in front of my house. He asked if he
3

could have (a, an) drink of water from our hose. He told me he moved here
4

because his mom got (a, an) new job. She is (a, an) architect. That means she
5   6

designs houses. He will go to (a, the) same school as I do. He's coming back
7

to have dinner with us in (a, an) hour.
8

Proofreading Practice:
Articles

As you read the article below, you will notice that some articles have been used incorrectly. Read the sentences carefully. Circle the articles that are incorrect. Then write the correct articles above the words you circled.

Twisters

Tornadoes, commonly called twisters, happen all over the world, but most occur in a United States. Usually 700 or more form each year in the U.S.

A twister is an funnel cloud. In the Northern Hemisphere, twisters rotate counterclockwise. In the Southern Hemisphere, they rotate clockwise.

A tornado forms when a warm air mass is pushed upward very quickly by an colder air mass. Then more warm air rushes in and starts to twist. The twisting warm winds suck even more warm air into the center of the cloud. The twisting grows more powerful until an funnel is formed.

Not all funnels touch the ground. When twisters do touch the earth's surface, the violent rotating winds can demolish almost everything in their path. A spinning winds can reach speeds of more than 200 miles per hour.

The best protection against an tornado is to take cover in a basement. If a basement is not available, crouching in a bathtub or under the sturdy piece of furniture away from windows is advised.

Recognizing Sentences

A sentence is a group of words that tells a whole idea.

- Look at the word groups below.

1	**2**
Kristie walked	Robin ran
3	**4**
crawled outside	Robin at the store

Write answers to the questions below.

1. Which word groups—1, 2, 3, and/or 4—would you say are complete sentences?

   _____

2. Which word groups are not complete sentences? _____

3. What are the subjects in word groups 1 and 2?

   _____   _____

4. What are the verbs in word groups 1 and 2?

   _____   _____

5. Does word group 3 contain a subject? _____

6. Does word group 4 contain a verb? _____

Think about how you answered the questions above. What two parts must a complete sentence have?

_____   _____

Recognizing Sentences

Read the following word groups. Write an *S* next to each complete sentence.
Write an *N* next to each word group that is not a complete sentence.

1. Hazel cooks _____

2. Walter the desk _____

3. The orange, red, and yellow flame _____

4. He walked quietly down the hill _____

5. Looking carefully through _____

6. The rain fell _____

7. Going to the fair _____

8. Lois jumped, and I yelled _____

9. He and the rhinoceros _____

10. The greatest day _____

A sentence begins with a capital letter and ends with a period, an exclamation point, or a question mark. Study these sentences.

Bruce nodded his head⊙   His eyes ˄closed slowly.   soon ˄he was asleep.

The sentences above have been proofread. As you have learned, *proofreading* means reading over what has been written and making corrections. Notice how the corrections above were made.

Proofread and correct the sentences below.

The cook stirred the mixture. then he poured it into a baking dish

He it into the oven. When do think it will be ready?

Completing Sentences

A sentence needs a good ending. Read the beginning of each sentence below. Write an ending to complete each sentence. Draw a picture of your complete sentence.

1. They won the important game with _____

   _____

   _____

   _____

2. We wanted it to snow so _____

   _____

   _____

   _____

3. The sky was filled with balloons _____

   _____

   _____

   _____

4. The smiling faces of the circus clowns turned

   to frowns when _____

   _____

   _____

   _____

Completing Sentences

A sentence needs a good ending. Read the ending of each sentence below. Write a beginning to complete each sentence. Draw a picture of your complete sentence.

1. _____

_____

_____

and ants soon found the food.

2. _____

_____

_____

because a dog followed me home from school.

3. _____

_____

_____

and suddenly I found myself falling.

4. _____

_____

_____

and then my alarm clock rang.

Writing Sentences

Look at each word. Write two words that tell something about the picture. Use the picture name and the two words to write a sentence about the picture.

1. ring

_____   _____

_____

_____

2. woman

_____   _____

_____

_____

3. mailman

_____   _____

_____

_____

4. socks

_____   _____

_____

_____

5. lizard

_____   _____

_____

_____

Types of Sentences
Statements, Questions, Exclamations, and Commands

- A statement is a sentence that simply gives information. It ends with a period.
    My teacher is Mr. Gonzales**.**

- A question asks for information; often begins with the words *who, what, when, where, why,* or *how*; and ends with a question mark.
    Who is Mr. Gonzales**?**

- Some statements sound like questions. Sentences that start with phrases like **I** *wonder* are usually not questions.
    I wonder who Mr. Gonzales is**.**

- An exclamation is a sentence that expresses a strong emotion, like fear, anger, or surprise. It ends with an exclamation point.
    You'll never guess where I saw Mr. Gonzales**!**

- A command is a sentence that asks someone to think or believe something. It can end with a period or with an exclamation point if you want to make it stronger.
    Tell me where you saw him**.** Quick, tell me**!**

- Using a variety of sentences makes it more interesting for your reader. You, as a writer, need to decide when to use each kind of sentence.

Practice

Next to each sentence, write its type: statement, question, exclamation, or command.

1. Have you ever met my friend Tina? _____

2. She is a wonderful person. _____

3. I can't say enough nice things about her! _____

4. Name one person who doesn't like her. _____

5. Call her today! _____

Statements from Questions

Write a statement in response to each question about you. Make sure each statement is a complete sentence.

1. What is your name? _____

2. When were you born? _____

3. Where were you born? _____

4. How much did you weigh? _____

5. How tall are you now? _____

6. What is your address? _____

7. What is the name of at least one neighbor? _____

_____

8. What time do you get up in the morning? _____

_____

9. What did you have for breakfast today? _____

_____

10. What do you usually do after dinner? _____

_____

11. What hobbies or interests do you have? _____

_____

12. Write a question about yourself. _____

Answer it. _____

Writing Different Types of Sentences

Use **only** the words in each box to write one of the four kinds of sentences. Use as many words in each sentence as you can. Some sentences will use more words than others. Some words may be used more than once, but not in the same sentence. However, all words must be used. Use correct punctuation.

Example:

in	where	pen	open	the	put	dog
don't		lives	live		does	his

STATEMENT: _____

QUESTION: _____

COMMAND: _____

EXCLAMATION: _____

money	class	who	the	sold	will	five	hundred	to
for	and	over		tickets	sell	school	make	

STATEMENT: _____

QUESTION: _____

COMMAND: _____

EXCLAMATION: _____

out	switch	the	is	by	watch	for
where		lights	stand	the	on	

STATEMENT: _____

QUESTION: _____

COMMAND: _____

EXCLAMATION: _____

Sentence Diary

Talk to your friends and family members. Write the complete sentences that you hear. Write the name of the speaker who used each sentence.

STATEMENTS   SPEAKER

_____   _____

_____   _____

_____   _____

_____   _____

QUESTIONS

_____   _____

_____   _____

_____   _____

_____   _____

COMMANDS

_____   _____

_____   _____

_____   _____

_____   _____

EXCLAMATIONS

_____   _____

_____   _____

_____   _____

_____   _____

Proofreading Practice:
Sentence Types

As you read the story below, you will notice that no punctuation has been used. Read the sentences carefully. Insert periods, question marks, and exclamation points where they are needed.

Sandwich Saga

How did the sandwich get its name In the early 1700s, a British nobleman called the Earl of Sandwich was playing cards with his friends He was hungry but he didn't want to stop playing He asked his servant to bring him a slice of meat between two pieces of bread Although bread and meat must have been eaten this way many times before, the Earl's eating the food this way made it fashionable and gave it a name The name "sandwich" caught on quickly and the sandwich's popularity spread

Today there are many kinds of sandwiches Some are served in long buns, such as hoagies, subs, or footlong hotdogs Others are stacked vertically, like double-decker hamburgers, triple-decker club sandwiches, or dagwoods Some are even served in pocket bread, also called pita bread All of these and many more varieties share the name sandwich thanks to the Earl of Sandwich What an amazing story

Writing with Your Senses

A photographer can appeal to only one sense—sight. A good writer, however, through imagination, appeals to all the senses—**sight**, **hearing**, **smell**, **taste**, and **touch**.

Imagine that you are alone in the basement of an old house. The batteries of your flashlight have just gone dead. It is so dark that you cannot even see your own hand in front of your face. You must feel your way, step by step, through the dark basement, up the stairs, and out. What do you touch? Does anything brush against you? On the lines that follow, describe in detail four things that you feel as you try to get out of the house.

_____

_____

_____

_____

As you walk through the house you begin to hear sounds. Is it the wind or maybe an insect? Use your imagination to describe what you might hear in an empty house. Describe four sounds and tell where they come from.

_____

_____

_____

_____

Writing with Your Senses

Eventually you reach a door and escape outside. What sounds do you hear now? List four sounds you might hear outside the empty house.

_____

_____

_____

_____

After your adventure in the house, you are frightened and tired. Most of all you are hungry. You head right for home and raid the refrigerator. On the lines that follow, tell what you ate and how it tasted.

_____

_____

_____

_____

Write On Your Own

The sense of smell is the hardest sense to write about. Many people are not very aware of smells. Also, there aren't too many words to describe smells. Yet smell can change your mood—it can bring back memories, make you think of spring, or make you hungry. Take a walk in your imagination through your house or neighborhood. What smells do you remember? How would you describe them? On another sheet of paper, write a list of at least ten things your nose remembers. Then describe them in complete sentences.

Identifying Nouns

A noun is a word that tells who or what did the action or was acted upon by the verb in the sentence. *Book, school, desk, kids, teacher,* and *room* are all nouns, and each has a form to show plural, or more than one. People's names are nouns, too.

- One way to improve your writing is to be sure you have chosen just the right noun. Nouns tell your readers exactly what the sentence is about. Compare these sentences.
    I saw a **thing** in the sky. I saw a **meteor** in the sky.

- When you write, you should think about how you can make your nouns more specific. Say *gentleman* instead of *person* or *toddler* instead of *kid,* for example.

Practice

Circle the nouns in this paragraph.

Have you ever heard people say they saw a shooting star? Stars don't really shoot across the sky. "Shooting stars" are meteors. A meteor can be made up of rock or other materials. It becomes brighter when it comes into the atmosphere (a layer of gas) surrounding Earth. Meteors are like fireworks when they come into the sky. Most meteors turn to dust by the time they get to Earth. But if the meteor doesn't, it is called a meteorite. The largest known meteorite on Earth is in Africa. It weighs 55 tons! Another meteorite made a crater in Canada more than 2 miles in diameter.

Identifying Nouns

Practice

Look at this sentence: **I saw something**. Use your imagination to write some nouns you could use instead of "something."

_____

_____

_____

Revise

Read the paragraph. Write a more specific noun above each underlined noun.

Thanksgiving is my favorite <u>day</u> of the year. Early in the day, my sister and I

₁

set the table. We put <u>things</u> at each place. Then we arrange <u>decorations</u> for a

₂ ₃

centerpiece. Mom is busy in the <u>room</u> preparing the <u>food</u>. <u>People</u> arrive just

₄ ₅ ₆

before three o'clock. After dinner, we play <u>games</u>. We end the celebration with

₇

a big helping of Grandma's special <u>dessert</u>!

₈

Writing More Exact Nouns

What's wrong with the ad below?

Well, a boat can be a beautiful new ocean liner or a dumpy old rowboat. Before you pay five hundred dollars, you'd probably want to know exactly what kind of boat you'd be traveling on. A more **exact noun**, like rowboat, gives more information than a general noun, like boat.

Read the following sentences. Replace each underlined general noun by writing an exact noun on the lines. You can use your own exact noun or choose one from the list below.

Saint Bernard	sports car	daisies
fruit salad	shriek	

1. The <u>animal</u> saved the little girl's life by keeping her warm during the snowstorm.

_____

2. The field shimmered with <u>flowers</u>. _____

_____

Writing More Exact Nouns
(Continued)

3. That <u>food</u> tasted good. _____

4. Suddenly a <u>sound</u> rang out in the night. _____

5. Ted drove up in his new <u>vehicle</u>. _____

For every general noun below, write two more exact nouns. The first one has been done for you.

1. animal   _____ **kangaroo** _____   _____ **robin** _____

2. clothes   _____   _____

3. furniture   _____   _____

4. snack   _____   _____

5. feeling   _____   _____

Rewrite the following paragraph. Replace each underlined noun or noun phrase with a more exact noun or noun phrase.

These two <u>guys</u> went hiking one day. <u>One guy</u> walked into <u>this place</u> and saw <u>this thing</u> peering through the trees. They just stared at each other for <u>some time</u>. <u>The other guy</u> dropped his <u>stuff</u> and took off. <u>The first guy</u> jumped and screamed, and <u>another person came</u> and scared it away.

_____

_____

_____

_____

_____

_____

Writing More Exact Nouns

Read the sentences. Look at the underlined nouns. Use more exact nouns to rewrite the sentences to make them more interesting. The first one is done for you.

1. The <u>bird</u> sang in the tree.

   <u>The cardinal sang in the tree.</u>

2. The <u>animal</u> built a nest.

   _____

3. The <u>people</u> roller skated in the park.

   _____

4. The <u>lady</u> baked cookies for the bake sale.

   _____

5. The <u>vehicle</u> broke down just outside of town.

   _____

6. The <u>man</u> served the food promptly.

   _____

7. The <u>flowers</u> grew right outside my bedroom window.

   _____

8. The <u>tree</u> blew over in the storm.

   _____

9. The <u>person</u> broke his arm.

   _____

Identifying Pronouns

Pronouns can be handy. They take the place of a noun, so you can say *he, she, it, they, her, him, them,* and so on without naming the same person, place, thing, or idea over and over again. But be careful! If you use pronouns too much, your reader might be confused.

- Read the sentence below. What is the problem with the use of the pronoun *she*?
  When Mom talked to Beckie today, she was angry.

- In this example, it is not clear who was angry, Mom or Beckie. One way to fix the problem is to replace *she* with the noun.
  When Mom talked to Beckie today, **Mom** was angry.

- Another way to fix the problem is to rearrange the words.
  Mom was angry when she talked to Beckie today.

Practice

Rewrite each sentence so that it is clear to whom or what the underlined pronoun refers.

1. Dad and Jack invited <u>his</u> cousins to visit.

_____

2. When Latrice and J. J. got there, <u>she</u> was tired.

_____

3. We offered them lemonade, juice, or soda. They said they wanted some of <u>that</u>.

_____

4. When our friends came, I asked Dad and Jack if <u>they</u> wanted some lunch.

_____

Identifying Pronouns

Practice

Write a paragraph about a hobby that you share or sport you play with a group of friends. Tell something about each of your friends. Do not use any pronouns. Circle words that can be replaced with pronouns.

_____

_____

_____

Revise

Write a pronoun above each underlined word or phrase.

People all over the world are trying to find more sources of energy that will reduce pollution. <u>People</u> are also trying to conserve fossil fuels by using renewable resources. Owen Fisher uses solar panels to heat his home in Arizona. <u>Owen</u> has installed solar panels on the roof to collect the sun's rays. <u>The sun's rays</u> are then converted directly into electricity. Amanda Perez has several windmills on her Nebraska farm. <u>Amanda</u> uses the wind's energy to generate electricity. Tom and Cathy Clark change the energy in a waterfall into electricity to run their mill in northern Maine. This source of natural power has saved <u>the Clarks</u> thousands of dollars. Water power is a clean, reusable source of energy, but <u>water power</u> often requires the construction of costly dams. Some people use <u>geothermal energy</u> to heat buildings. Geothermal energy comes from the hot, molten rock in Earth's core.

Identifying Adjectives

An adjective is a word that describes a noun or a pronoun. *Kind, generous,* and *helpful* are all adjectives that describe friend in the example above. An adjective is a word that usually can fit in both these blanks:

The _____ tree is very _____.

Adjectives give readers more information about a subject. There is a big difference between a *kind friend* and a *fake friend.*

- Adjectives usually come before the words they describe.
    a **funny** friend   a **happy** friend

- Like nouns and verbs, adjectives work best when they are specific. Which adjective in the sentences below tells you more about Maria?
    Maria is **nice**.   Maria is **generous**.

When you write, try to use adjectives that give the reader a clear idea.

Practice

Underline the nineteen adjectives in the paragraph.

I peered out my window into the dark, deserted street. A pale, yellow streetlight cast a fuzzy glow onto the sidewalk. A policeman, with a shiny badge pinned to his navy, blue uniform, made his usual rounds. Our friendly neighbor, on his way to his demanding job, dashed out of the building and let the heavy door slam behind him. A jet-black cat sped across the sidewalk and into the darkness. I looked again at the crescent moon and got into my bed. Just as I was about to pull my soft, warm, faded quilt over my tired body, I heard a faint sound.

Identifying Adjectives

Practice

Write the next paragraph of the story on the previous page. What do you think this person heard? Use at least six adjectives that show what it looked like, sounded like, moved like, maybe even smelled like.

_____

_____

_____

_____

_____

_____

Revise

Write a more interesting adjective above each underlined adjective.

It was a <u>nice</u> day in July. We packed a <u>good</u> lunch and bicycled over to ?nyhill
    1   2

Beach. We could hardly wait to jump into the <u>cool</u> water. <u>Some</u> umbrell? ?otted
                        3   4

the sand. <u>Nervous</u> mothers and <u>moving</u> toddlers lined the water's ed? ?he
        5   6

<u>happy</u> swimmers raced out to the <u>big</u> raft. Several <u>small</u> sailboats circled the lake.
7   8   9

It was a <u>great</u> day!
      10

Writing More Exact Adjectives

The man in the picture just sold you a radio that doesn't work. You want to warn your friends. How would you describe the man? Jot down a few adjectives on the following lines.

_____

_____

_____

_____

_____

You probably know that describing him as "some guy" won't help. You want to use more exact adjectives so your friends can picture him clearly in their minds. Try to use **exact adjectives** whenever you write a description.

Look at the pair of adjectives in each of the following sentences. Underline the more specific adjective.

1. The man had a (rasping, funny) voice.

2. He had a (weird, dangerous) look in his eye.

3. The man's jacket was (crumpled, old looking).

4. His movements were (strange, jerky).

5. His (choppy, peculiar) manner of speaking made me feel (nervous, bad).

Writing More Exact Adjectives

Read the paragraph. It's about the farmhouse in the picture below.

> It was a <u>nice</u>, <u>old</u> farmhouse built over a <u>pretty</u> brook. Next to the house was a lovely meadow with <u>fantastic</u> flowers everywhere. The house was a <u>wonderful</u> building with <u>neat</u> <u>little</u> windows and doors.

We know from the sample paragraph that the writer liked the farmhouse, but we don't know what the farmhouse looked like. Rewrite the paragraph on the lines below. Look at the picture and choose exact adjectives that describe what you see.

_____

_____

_____

_____

_____

_____

Identifying Adverbs

- An **adverb** is a word that describes a verb, adjective, or even another adverb. This adverb describes the adjective *long*.

    It was a **very** long book.

- Like adjectives, adverbs give your reader more information. Adverbs usually tell *how* something is done. They often end *in* -ly, as in *quickly, quietly,* and *happily*.

    Steve chose his book **carefully**.

- Adverbs can often be placed in several different places in a sentence. This adverb describes the verb *finished*.

    Steve **quickly finished** his book.
    Quickly, Steve **finished** his book.
    Steve **finished** his book **quickly**.

- Some writers use the adverb *very* too much. When a word is used too often, it loses its meaning for your reader. Look at these other words to use or other ways to say *very*.

    Steve is **very** smart.   Steve is extremely smart.
    He reads **very** much.   He is an avid reader.

- Many writers confuse the adverb well with the adjective *good*. Here they are used correctly.

    Steve is a **good** student.   (an adjective describing **student**)
    He does **well** in school.   (an adverb telling **how**)

Practice

Complete each sentence with an adverb that best fits in the sentence.

The teacher _____ passed back the papers. Eric wasn't doing very
                              1

_____ in the class. He _____ looked at his paper. He
            2   3

_____ showed his A paper to his friend.
            4

Identifying Adverbs

Practice

Fill in each blank with an adverb of your own.

Trish was taking her dog Beast for a walk. Something black and white ambled _____ out from under the bushes. Beast stopped and began to growl _____. Trish took one look and _____ ran back to the house. Beast _____ walked home. Trish _____ led Beast out into the yard and sprayed him off with the garden hose. She _____ scolded her pet, "Beast, you must _____ learn to stay away from skunks!"

Revise

Add an adverb to each sentence. Remember that adverbs can often be placed in several different places in a sentence.

Example: The mother cat licked her baby.
lovingly

The wind and the sun were discussing who was stronger. A traveler walked down the road. The sun said, "Whoever can make the traveler remove his cloak will be the stronger one." The wind began to blow on the traveler. The traveler wrapped his cloak around himself. The wind gave up. The sun shone. The traveler found it too hot to wear his cloak. The wind had to admit that the sun was the stronger one.

Writing More Exact Adverbs

- **Adverbs** tell how, when, or where something happens. Gino is singing <u>loudly</u> <u>in the shower</u> <u>now.</u>

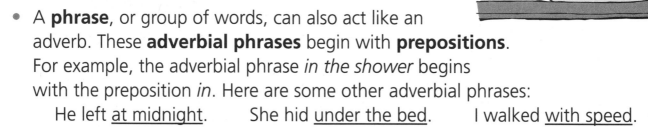

- An adverb can be a single word, such as *loudly* or *now*. Many adverbs are formed from adjectives by adding *ly*:
  loud loud<u>ly</u>   fond fond<u>ly</u>   slow slow<u>ly</u>

- A **phrase**, or group of words, can also act like an adverb. These **adverbial phrases** begin with **prepositions**. For example, the adverbial phrase *in the shower* begins with the preposition *in*. Here are some other adverbial phrases:
  He left <u>at midnight</u>.   She hid <u>under the bed</u>.   I walked <u>with speed</u>.

Complete the following sentences by writing an adverb or an adverbial phrase which answers the question in parentheses.

1. I told my brother I'd go to the museum _____.
(when?)

2. That knight's armor is standing _____.
(where?)

3. I like the way it shines so _____.
(how?)

4. I see many paintings _____.
(where?)

5. I don't mind being with my little brother, he usually acts _____.
(how?)

6. We will go to the library _____.
(when?)

Writing More Exact Adverbs

- You can use adverbs to answer more than one question in a sentence. For example:
    Joanna was swimming. (*Where* and *when* was she swimming?)
    Joanna was swimming underwater at three o'clock.

- You can also vary the position of the adverbs in a sentence. For example:
    At three o'clock, Joanna was swimming underwater.

Rewrite each of the following sentences on the lines below. Add an adverb that answers the question in parentheses.

1. Oscar plays the trombone. (How and where does he play it?)

_____

_____

2. Mr. Lopez found the box. (Where and when did he find it?)

_____

_____

3. The dog has disappeared! (How and when did it disappear?)

_____

_____

Verbs
Regular and Irregular

- A **verb** is a word that tells about something that happens. To make a verb tell about something that happened in the past, you usually add *-ed*.

  We **walk** to the park.   We **walked** to the park.

- If the verb ends in *e*, you don't need another e. just add a *-d*.

  We **share** popcorn.   We **shared** popcorn.

- If the verb ends in *y*, you usually change the *y* to an *i* and add *-ed*.

  We **carry** our lunch.   We **carried** our lunch.

- Many verbs do not follow these rules. They are irregular.

- Most irregular verbs would not sound right if you tried to add *-ed*.
  We **run** up the grassy hill.   We **ran** up the grassy hill.
  We **eat** our lunch.   We **ate** our lunch.

- Here are some irregular verbs in the present and past tense:

Present	Past	Present	Past	Present	Past
buy	bought	fall	fell	is	was
do	did	find	found	see	saw
draw	drew	get	got	sit	sat
drink	drank	give	gave	stand	stood
drive	drove	go	went	write	wrote

Practice

Write the correct past-tense verb above each underlined verb.

1. I <u>sit</u> under a tree at the park.

2. I <u>watch</u> children playing basketball.

3. I <u>draw</u> pictures of the children.

4. I <u>try</u> to make each picture perfect.

Verbs
Regular and Irregular

Proofread

There are ten mistakes in forming the past tense in this paragraph. Use the proofreader's mark (⌿) to delete each incorrect verb and write the correct verb above it.

Example: They ~~gived~~ *gave* me a ticket to the concert.

> Maria sitted very still. She seed the other performers waiting and wondered if they were nervous, too. She try to think about other things. She was glad her mother braid her long, brown hair this morning. Maria even getted to wear her favorite dress, the one her mom buyed her for her birthday. As she listen to the first child play, Maria felt more relaxed. The music sound lovely, and the girl felt happy and excited to be there. Finally, it be her turn. She goed onto the stage and played her very best.

Write On Your Own

On a separate sheet of paper, write five sentences that tell about something that has already happened. You may choose to write about a family trip, a day you spent with a friend, or you may choose your own idea. Remember to put the verbs in the past tense.

Verbs
Using Past-Tense Forms

On the line in each sentence that follows, write the past tense of the verb in parentheses. Use your dictionary to check on irregular forms if you need help.

1. Alicia and I (try) _____ to move the piano the other day.

2. We accidentally (break) _____ an expensive lamp.

3. Alicia (scrape) _____ the paint off the wall and (rip) _____ the carpet.

4. I (trip) _____ and (sprain) _____ my ankle.

5. The piano leg (fall) _____ through the floor.

6. The noise (bother) _____ my uncle, who was sleeping in the room below.

7. He (dream) _____ that he was on a ship.

8. He (think) _____ that an iceberg hit the ship.

9. So he (grab) _____ a pillow and (jump) _____ overboard.

10. He (awake) _____ on the floor.

Verbs
Using Past-Tense Forms

- Look at the underlined verbs in the following sentences.
    Dad <u>has worked</u> for the city for twenty years.
    I <u>have sampled</u> all thirty-two flavors of ice cream.

- Notice that *has* and *have* are followed by forms of verbs that look like the past tense (*worked, sampled*). For regular verbs, the form following *have* is the same as the past-tense form. But many irregular verbs have different forms after *have*. Here are a few. You will find others listed in your dictionary.

Verb	Past	Form After <u>Have</u>
come	came	come
eat	ate	eaten
go	went	gone
ring	rang	rung

Write in the correct past-tense form of the verb in parentheses for each sentence below. Use a dictionary if you need help.

1. Bjorn has _____ you a present. (bring)

2. Aunt May has _____ your favorite cake. (make)

3. Have you _____ it yet? (see)

4. Why haven't you _____ me about it? (tell)

5. The ball has _____ the window. (break)

6. Susie has _____ to try out for the class play. (decide)

7. What has Chita _____ under the bed? (hide)

8. Have you or your sister _____ on an airplane? (fly)

Verbs
Subject-Verb Agreement

- Every sentence has a subject and a verb. Present-tense verbs have two forms: the **plain form**, like *play*, and the **s form**, like *plays*. The verb form must go with, or *agree* with, the subject. Look at these examples.

  Gloria <u>plays</u> softball.　　　　　The girls <u>play</u> softball.
  She <u>plays</u> softball.　　　　　　I <u>play</u> softball.
  Gloria and Juan <u>play</u> softball.　　You <u>play</u> softball.
  They <u>play</u> softball.　　　　　　We <u>play</u> softball.

Use the sentences above to help you complete the following generalizations.

1. When the subject is a singular noun or the pronoun *it, she, or he,* use the

   _____ form of the verb.

2. When the subject is a plural noun, two nouns joined by *and,* or the pronoun *I, you,*

   we, or *they,* use the _____ form of the verb.

To make the *s* form of most verbs, you add *s* or *es*. Some verbs change form slightly.
　　do　　do<u>es</u>　　　bury　　bur<u>ies</u>　　　have　　h<u>as</u>

Underline the correct form of the present-tense verb in the following sentences.

1. Every day I (jog, jogs) along the river.

2. My sister (run, runs) five miles before school.

3. She (go, goes) around the park five times.

4. My two spaniels (scurry, scurries) next to me most of the way.

5. Then they (take, takes) off after a cat or a bicycle.

6. Two police officers always (pass, passes) us.

7. They (smile, smiles) and (wave, waves) at us.

Verbs
Subject-Verb Agreement

- The word **be** has some special present-tense forms:

  I <u>am</u> singing. You <u>are</u> singing. He <u>is</u> singing.

  We <u>are</u> singing. The girls <u>are</u> singing. They <u>are</u> singing.

Fill in the blank with the correct present-tense form of **be**.

1. I _____ going to the movies tonight.

2. Tom _____ coming with me.

3. We _____ taking the bus downtown.

4. Philip and Chris _____ meeting us there.

5. Terry, you _____ welcome to come, too.

Write On Your Own

Write a short diary entry for your favorite TV or book character. Tell what you think she or he might be doing or thinking now. Use present-tense verb forms. Underline each verb form you use.

Verbs
Subject-Verb Agreement

Review:

The *subject* of a sentence tells whom or what the sentence is about. The *verb* tells what the subject does or is. The subject and verb have to agree—the verb has to be in the correct form.

- If the subject is a singular noun, or *he, she,* or *it,* add *-s* to the verb.
  The bus **comes** through our neighborhood.
  It usually **runs** on time.

- If the subject is a plural noun, or *I, we , you,* or *they,* do not add *-s* to the verb.
  Many kids **walk** to school.
  I **walk** to school every day.
  We all **walk** together.

- If the verb ends in *o, sh, ch,* or *s,* add *-es* instead of *-s.*
  Ricky **wishes** he could ride his bike to school.
  I **do**, too. He **does** a lot of complaining.

- If the verb ends in *y,* change the *y* to *i* and add *-es.*
  I **try** to convince my mom that it would be okay.
  He **tries**, too, but she thinks we should go together.

- There are some common verbs that do not follow these rules.
  | I **have** | we **have** | he **has** |
  | I **am** | we **are** | he **is** |

Practice

Fill in each blank with a present-tense verb that agrees with the subject.

1. (to eat) She _____.

2. (to bring) He _____.

3. (to talk) Rosa _____.

4. (to be) Susan _____.

5. (to fall) It _____.

6. (to like) He _____.

Verbs
Subject-Verb Agreement

Proofread

There are seven errors in subject-verb agreement in this paragraph. Use the proofreader's mark (✍) to delete each incorrect word and write the correct word above it.

Example: My sister and I keeps the same schedule.

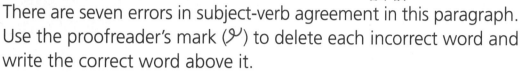

After school every day, my sister and I walk home together. Our mom call us from work to make sure we are home and safe. I finish my homework and help my sister while she do her homework. Then we have a snack. I make the snack, and my sister clean the dishes. My mom usually leave a list of chores for us to do after our homework is done. Every Monday my sister fold laundry and I helps her put it away. We're always glad when my mom get home from work!

Practice

Write five sentences telling what members of your family do to help out in your home. What chores do you do? What do other family members do?

_____

_____

_____

_____

_____

Verbs
Subject-Verb Agreement

- When the subject is first and the verb comes right after it, it is easy to be sure the verb is in the right form.

  I like to go to the rodeo.
  Terry likes to go, too.

- The subject is not always followed by the verb. No matter where the verb is, you still need to make it agree with the subject. Notice that in these examples, the verb comes *before* the subject.

  Have you ever been to the rodeo?
  Has your cousin ever been invited to come, too?

- Sometimes the subject and verb are separated by a phrase that gives more information about the subject.

  My cousin from Dallas always **comes** to see the rodeo.

When you are revising, look at every verb and its subject, wherever it is. Be sure they agree.

Practice

The subject and verb in each sentence are underlined.
Rewrite each sentence so that the subject and verb agree.

1. <u>Has</u> <u>you</u> ever looked through a telescope?

   _____

2. The <u>telescope</u> in Rosa's apartment <u>are</u> powerful.

   _____

3. The <u>stars</u> in the sky <u>sparkles</u> like diamonds.

   _____

4. I wonder what an <u>astronaut</u> traveling through space <u>see</u>.

   _____

Verbs
Subject-Verb Agreement

Practice

Choose a word or phrase from each column
and combine them to write at least five sentences.
Be sure your subjects and verbs agree.

the kids	at our school	is	happy
a girl	on my block	are	playing
the dogs	from next door	look	friendly
my friend	on TV	looks	angry
the teacher	in the cartoon	seems	tall

1. _____

_____

2. _____

_____

3. _____

_____

4. _____

_____

5. _____

_____

Proofreading Practice:
Subject-Verb Agreement

As you read the article below, you will notice that there are errors in subject-verb agreement. Read the sentences carefully. Use the proofreader's mark (℘) to delete the incorrect verbs. Then write the correct verbs above them.

The Origin of Football

American football develop from the game of soccer. In many foreign countries, soccer are called football. Football was first played in the eastern part of the United States in the mid-1800s. It was mostly a kicking game. The primary way goals was scored was to kick the ball over the opponent's goal line. Often thirty players plays on a team at once.

Over the years, many of the rules changes. Some rules were intended to help the teams score in other ways, like carrying the ball over the goal line. Running, tackling, and blocking was the main elements of football in the 1900s. The forward pass became popular around 1913 and adds excitement to the game. It also helped to eliminate some of the injuries caused from the tackling brawls of early football. Today football are one of the most popular sports in America.

Writing More Exact Verbs

Review:

- A verb tells what the person, place, idea, or thing in a sentence is doing, or it links or connects the subject to the rest of the sentence. A verb might tell about being rather than acting, as in this sentence.

    The sun **is** hot.

- Compare the verbs in these two sentences below.
  Which verb gives you a better picture of what happened?

    The plate **fell** to the floor.
    The plate **crashed** to the floor.

Crashed is a better choice for this sentence because it tells the reader exactly how the plate fell—with a crash!

When you write, decide exactly what you want your reader to know. Then choose your verbs carefully to get your message across.

Practice

Underline the verb in each sentence. In the space after each sentence, write a word from the word bank that could replace the verb to make the sentence more powerful.

scribbled	gazed	announced	flip
leaped	blasted	slammed	sped

1. She hit the ball out of the park. _____

2. His bike went down the hill. _____

3. Turn over the pancake. _____

4. She jumped over the fence. _____

5. He looked at the trophy. _____

6. She played her radio. _____

7. He said his name. _____

8. He wrote a note. _____

Writing More Exact Verbs

Practice

Write three simple sentences to tell something that
happened today. For example, you might write: I got out
of bed. I ate breakfast. I walked to school.

_____

_____

_____

Choose two or three verbs from your sentences. Write them in the column on the left.
On the right, write your ideas for more powerful verbs. Can you think of a verb that tells
how something was done? What else do you want your reader to know?

First-draft verbs   **Better verbs**

_____   _____

_____   _____

_____   _____

Revise

Write a more exact verb above the underlined word(s) to improve the paragraph.

Just before I <u>got on</u> the plane, I <u>looked</u> up at the sky. It was full of dark,
₁   ₂

threatening clouds. I <u>put on</u> my seat belt and <u>held</u> the armrests as the plane took
₃   ₄

off. I <u>looked</u> at the other passengers. No one else seemed nervous. Just then a
₅

bolt of lightning <u>happened</u> right next to my window. The pilot <u>said</u> that our ride
₆   ₇

might be bumpy. I knew I should have taken the train!

Writing More Exact Verbs

A good writer chooses verbs carefully. To express an idea well, a writer should use an **exact verb**.

Think of one or more verbs that could be used instead of *walked* in the following sentence to express the ideas below. The first one has been done to get you started.

The girl <u>walked</u> down the street.

1. happiness __skipped, pranced_____

2. haste _____

3. clumsiness _____

4. pain _____

5. tiredness _____

Write more exact verbs for the verb said in the following sentence to express the ideas below.

The boy <u>said</u>, "I did it."

1. loudness _____

2. sadness _____

3. softness _____

4. happiness _____

5. confusion _____

Writing More Exact Verbs

Your writing will be more interesting and more accurate if you use one exact verb instead of a general verb helped by an adverb. For example:

Butch, Slim, and I <u>walked slowly</u> past Creely's dump.
Butch, Slim, and I <u>trudged</u> past Creely's dump.

Think of one exact verb to replace the underlined verb and adverb in the sentences below.

1. "Such a dull summer," Butch <u>said unhappily</u>. _____

2. Just then Elly Moss's time machine <u>came noisily</u> into sight. _____

3. Its silver and glass discs <u>shone brightly</u> in the sun. _____

4. In a second we were <u>moving quickly</u> after it. _____

5. The time machine landed on the courthouse lawn; we were <u>looking carefully</u>

   at the cockpit. _____

6. The cockpit slid open, and Elly Moss and a strange creature <u>came quickly</u> out of the

   machine. _____

7. "I'm just back from the twenty-third century," Elly <u>said loudly</u>, "and do I have news

   for you!" _____

Proofreading Practice:
Exact Verbs

As you read the report below, you will notice that some
of the verbs are underlined. Read the sentences carefully.
Replace each underlined verb with an exact, more interesting verb.
For extra practice, use the proofreader's mark (≡) to correct
the errors in capitalization.

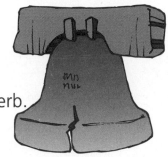

Liberty Bell

Why is a bell that no longer rings so famous? The silent bell <u>is</u> in Liberty Bell

Pavilion in philadelphia, pennsylvania. Many people come to view this symbol of

liberty.

Before pennsylvania <u>was</u> a state, the people living there had the liberty bell

<u>made</u> in england and shipped to philadelphia. It was rung along with church bells

to <u>tell of</u> the signing of the declaration of independence. It <u>broke</u> while it was

ringing but was soon fixed.

For more than 80 years philadelphians rang it every fourth of july. Then it

cracked again when it was rung during the funeral of a famous judge, john

marshall. The bell was not repaired. It has never rung again, but it is <u>saved</u> as a

symbol of independence for all of the citizens of the united states.

Comparisons

When we **compare** things, we look for ways in which they are similar and ways in which they are different. One way to compare different things is to tell how they look, feel, sound, smell, or taste. We use **adjectives** to make such comparisons.

List the adjectives from the picture above.

_____   _____

_____   _____

Comparisons

Notice that we change short adjectives that compare two items by adding **er** at the end. We use **more** in front of longer adjectives when we compare two items.

Write a sentence with an adjective to compare each pair below.

1. a baseball and a basketball: _____

_____

2. a flower and a weed: _____

_____

3. a pencil and a typewriter: _____

_____

- When we use adjectives to compare more than two items, we add **est** to short adjectives. We use the word **most** in front of longer adjectives.
  Of the three kittens, Snowball has the <u>whitest</u> fur.
  But Tiger is the <u>most playful</u> of the three.

Choose one of the groups below. Write three or more sentences using adjectives to compare the different members of the group.
   an apple, a cherry, and a banana
   a mouse, a dog, and an elephant
   a skateboard, a bike, and a car

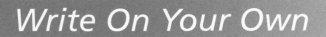

_____

_____

_____

Write On Your Own

Think of two TV characters, two places, or two meals to compare. Choose one that you like a lot and one that you don't like. Then, on another sheet of paper, write five sentences comparing the two. Try to use an *er* or more adjective in each sentence in your paragraph.

Writing Comparisons Correctly

As you have learned, an adjective is a word that describes a noun, which is often a person, place, or thing.

- Sometimes you will want to compare two people, places, or things. You can usually do this by adding **-er** to the adjective that describes them.
  My uncle is **taller** than my dad.

- If there are more than two subjects, add **-est** to the adjective.
  My aunt is taller than both of her brothers. She is the **tallest**.

- With longer adjectives, it sounds better to use **more** and **most**.
  She is **more athletic** than Uncle Bob.
  She is the **most athletic** of all my relatives.

- The words **good** and **bad** are special words.
  You do not add **-er** and **-est** or use **more** or **most**.
  My dad's spaghetti sauce is **good**.
  His macaroni and cheese is **better**.
  His noodle soup is the **best**.

  My aunt's tuna casserole is **bad**.
  Her meat loaf is **worse**.
  Her green bean salad is the **worst**.

Practice

For each sentence, choose the correct word or phrase in the parentheses and write it in the blank.

1. This winter was the _____ winter of the century. (coldest, most cold)

2. It snowed _____ this year, too. (harder, more hard)

3. Grandfather said it was the _____ winter he had ever seen. (baddest, worst)

4. The _____ thing about winter is the sledding. (best, goodest)

5. The _____ hill is right behind our house. (most awesome, awesomest)

Writing Comparisons Correctly

Proofread

This paragraph has five mistakes in adjectives that compare. Use the proofreader's mark (⌒) to delete the incorrect word or words and write the correct word or words above them.

Example: There are ~~badder~~ *worse* things than losing a race.

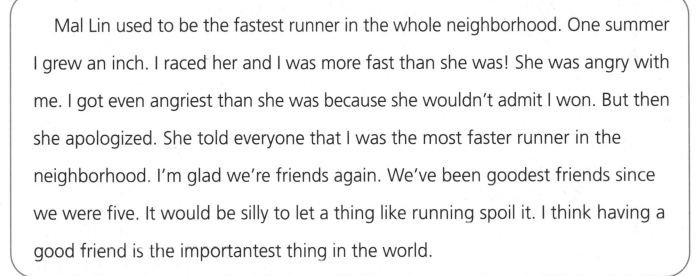

Mal Lin used to be the fastest runner in the whole neighborhood. One summer I grew an inch. I raced her and I was more fast than she was! She was angry with me. I got even angriest than she was because she wouldn't admit I won. But then she apologized. She told everyone that I was the most faster runner in the neighborhood. I'm glad we're friends again. We've been goodest friends since we were five. It would be silly to let a thing like running spoil it. I think having a good friend is the importantest thing in the world.

Practice

Write four sentences comparing the people in the picture above.

_____

_____

_____

_____

_____

Proofreading Practice:
Comparisons

As you read the article below, you will notice that some of the adjectives used to compare have not been used correctly. Read the sentences carefully. Cross out the comparisons that are incorrect. Write the correct adjective above the words you circled.

Fun in the Sun

Florida could be called the "Funshine State" as well as the "Sunshine State." Many people vacation there, because of the warm, sunny climate and the many interesting things to do there.

Near the center of the state, in Orlando, Florida, families flock to theme parks, such as Walt Disney World and Sea World. On the west coast at Tampa is another park, Busch Gardens, which features exhibits of rare birds, African animals, and tropical plants. More further south is Florida's most largest lake, Lake Okeechobee, which covers about 680 square miles. The Everglades and Big Cypress Swamp spread over mostest of southern Florida. Sports fans might want to visit Miami, the home of the Orange Bowl. At the extreme southern tip of Florida are the Florida Keys, made up of small islands which curve southwest for 150 miles. Key Largo is the larger of all these islands and is a popular vacation spot.

Writing Similes

- A **simile** is a comparison that uses the words **like** or **as**. These words clearly show that a comparison is being made.

      Anita's hair is **as** curly **as** lamb's wool.

      Cutting her hair was **like** shearing a sheep.

Find five similes in these lines from "A Visit from Saint Nicholas." Then on the lines below, write what is being compared in each simile.

His eyes, how they twinkled! His dimples, how merry!

His cheeks were like roses, his nose like a cherry!

And the beard on his chin was as white as the snow;

The stump of a pipe he held tight in his teeth,

And the smoke it encircled his head like a wreath;

He had a broad face and a little round belly,

That shook when he laughed like a bowl full of jelly.

—Clement Moore

Find five similes in these lines from "A Visit from Saint Nicholas." Then on the lines below, write what is being compared in each simile.

1. _____ are compared to _____.

2. _____ is compared to _____.

3. _____ is compared to _____.

4. _____ is compared to _____.

5. _____ is compared to_____.

Similes can make our spoken and written language more colorful. Frequently similes are funny or descriptive. Here are two ways to say the same thing.

      He was very happy.

      He was as happy as a mosquito at a crowded beach.

Writing Similes

Complete the following similes. Try to think of fresh and different comparisons.

1. clumsy as _____

2. hot as _____

3. Your suit looks like _____

4. She plays tennis as if _____

5. as nervous as _____

6. a laugh like _____

7. He walks like _____

Now write similes that describe two of the following situations. Use the lines below.

the cafeteria during lunchtime   a blizzard
waking up from a nightmare   the last day of summer vacation

_____

_____

_____

_____

Write On Your Own

The following poem is made up of similes.

> My grandmother was tall, like the sunflowers near the porch.
> Her eyes were gray, like the granite walls of the courthouse.
> My grandmother was strong, like the tree roots which push up sidewalks.

On another sheet of paper, write your own simile poem. First, think about someone or something you have strong feelings for—a member of your family, a friend, a pet, your home. Next, decide what you will compare the person or thing with. Finally, write your comparisons in a series of similes.

Writing Similes

- Sometimes to create a stronger mental picture, two unlike things are compared.
  The boy walked <u>slowly</u>. A turtle is <u>slow.</u>
  The boy walked like a turtle.

  The boy and turtle are compared. Slowness is what they have in common. Comparisons such as these are called **similes**.

Read the sentences below. A word (or words) is underlined in each one. Think about that word and of what other thing that word might be characteristic. Rewrite the sentence and make a comparison using **like** or **as** to connect the two things. Be creative.

1. The wind blew **in a circle**. _____

2. The sly fox watched his next meal **quietly** from behind the rock.

   _____

3. The morning was **crisp** after the storm.

   _____

4. The road was **narrow and winding**.

   _____

5. Chad walked **proudly** onto the stage to receive the award.

   _____

6. The snow fell **silently** on the roof.

   _____

7. Paper flew **up** around the room when the window was opened.

   _____

8. The boy was **mean** when he did not get what he wanted.

   _____

Writing Metaphors

- A **metaphor** compares two things without using like or as. A metaphor uses a word or phrase which means one thing to describe another.

  This classroom is a zoo.

  The ghost of a moon slipped behind the trees and disappeared.

Tell what two things are being compared in each metaphor above.

1. _____

2. _____

Metaphors can help readers see things in new ways. Metaphors add color and imagination to writing.

Look at the pictures below. What do they remind you of? On the lines at the top of the next page, write a metaphor to describe each picture.

1.

2.

Writing Metaphors

1. _____

_____

2. _____

_____

What do the following things remind you of? Using metaphors, write sentences about four of the items on the lines below.

| a spring day | a difficult math problem | an old, worn-out car |
| a stingy person | a garbage dump | an alarm clock |

1. _____

_____

2. _____

_____

3. _____

_____

4. _____

_____

Write On Your Own

A metaphor can be just one sentence. Or a whole paragraph can extend the metaphor and explain it. For example:

> Grace was a walking tape recorder. She was the nosiest person in the school. Her ears were microphones. She seemed to have a special sense that could pick up a piece of hot gossip at the other end of the cafeteria. She heard—and remembered—everything.

Choose one of the metaphors you wrote for above, or think of another. On a separate sheet of paper, write a paragraph that extends and explains your metaphor.

Writing Metaphors

- Sometimes two things that are different, but have a characteristic in common, are compared to create a stronger mental image.

    The cook was a jewel.

The cook really was not a jewel, but he was so good that he was valuable like a jewel. Like or as were not used in this comparison. Such a comparison is called a **metaphor**. Metaphors may replace various parts of speech.

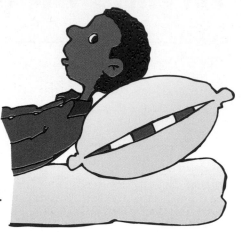

Underline the metaphors in the following sentences. Write what each metaphor means.

1. The pillow was a rock. _____

2. The heat crashed down on the highway workers. _____

3. She walked with lead in her shoes. _____

4. Chris was heartbroken when Sissy told him good-bye. _____

_____

Fill in the sentences with words from the box to create metaphors.

sandpaper	music to my ears	moaned
a rat's nest	eats tacks	cotton balls

1. Mr. Hubbard's cabinet under the sink was _____.

2. The news is _____.

3. The mounds of snow were _____.

4. In the winter my hands are _____.

5. The elevator _____ at the end of a long day's work.

6. Mr. Howard _____ for breakfast.

Similes and Metaphors

Rewrite the following simple sentences to make them more interesting or clearer. The first time, use adjectives and adverbs. The second time, use a simile or metaphor. You may need to rearrange some words.

1. The children cheered. _____

   _____

2. The sun blazed. _____

   _____

3. The geese honked. _____

   _____

4. The lions roared. _____

   _____

5. The cars sped. _____

   _____

6. The woman walked. _____

   _____

7. The man yelled. _____

   _____

8. The fish swam. _____

   _____

9. The radio blared. _____

   _____

10. The lamp glowed. _____

    _____

Polishing Your Writing

When you have finished writing, you should **proofread** your work to correct any errors in capitalization, commas, end punctuation, apostrophes, verb forms, and so on. You may also revise your work. To **revise** means to rewrite with improvements. When you revise, you may choose more exact nouns, verbs, or adjectives. You may add adverbial phrases. You may combine sentences to improve paragraph rhythm or to clarify your meaning.

Read the paragraph below. Rewrite the sentences using more exact nouns, adjectives, and adverbs. Be creative.

> The streets were crowded. They were narrow. We heard sounds filling the air. People went from store to store. Someone dropped a lot of packages. Many people rushed over to help. We all felt good.

_____

_____

_____

_____

_____

Polishing Your Writing

Revise the next paragraph yourself. Try to make each subject and verb exact. Use the tools you have learned to make the paragraph more interesting.

The car came down the street. It stopped. The man asked for directions. A woman was on the sidewalk. She had a dog. She told the man something. He drove away.

_____

_____

_____

_____

_____

Main Idea and Topic Sentences

Look at this picture.

What is the main idea of the picture? You might say that one fisherman caught a lot of fish but the other pulled up a rubber tire.

Paragraphs also have main ideas. The **main idea** of a paragraph is what the paragraph is all about. The **details** in the paragraph tell about the main idea.

Write a paragraph about the picture above. You already know the main idea.
Add some details to complete your paragraph.

_____

_____

_____

_____

_____

_____

Main Idea and Topic Sentences

Sometimes the main idea is stated in one sentence. This sentence is called the topic sentence. The **topic sentence** can be found anywhere in a paragraph, but usually it comes at the beginning or end of the paragraph. Do you have a topic sentence in your paragraph that you wrote on the previous page? If so, underline it.

Read the following paragraph. Underline the topic sentence.

Either the well was very deep, or Alice fell very slowly, for she had plenty of time as she went down to look about her and to wonder what was going to happen next. First, she tried to look down and make out what she was coming to, but it was too dark to see anything. Then she looked at the sides of the well and noticed that they were filled with cupboards and bookshelves. She took down a jar from one of the shelves as she passed. It was labeled "ORANGE MARMALADE," but to her great disappointment it was empty. She did not like to drop the jar for fear of killing somebody underneath, so she managed to put it into one of the cupboards as she fell past it.

—Lewis Carroll

Write On Your Own

On another sheet of paper, write a paragraph about the strangest thing you have ever seen. Experiment with where you place the topic sentence. Write the paragraph in three different ways. First, begin with the topic sentence. Next, end with the topic sentence. Finally, rewrite the paragraph with the topic sentence in the middle of the paragraph.

Topic Sentences

Read the following paragraphs. Decide what would make a
good topic sentence for each paragraph, Write it on the line above.

1. _____

The monkey shows are at 10:00 and 3:00 daily. The elephant show is performed on
weekends at 2:00. The seals perform Monday, Wednesday, and Saturday at 11:00 and at
1:00 on the other days of the week. The shows will continue until the end of the summer.

2. _____

The Miller's children are Mike, age eight, Sandra, five years old, and baby Emily, two months
old. They have a dog, Blackie, and a cat, Tiger. The house sometimes seems too small.

3. _____

Hunters wear long underwear, heavy sweaters, down vests, warm socks and boots, and
caps with earflaps. They have to dress warmly because they are out in the cold so long.
Their vests and caps are often a bright color so other hunters won't mistake them for
a deer.

4. _____

I could not sleep. The wind blew the rain against the window. The shutters beat against
the house: bang, bang, bang. Lightning lit up the room. I was happy but tired when morning
came. The storm had ended.

5. _____

Things were certainly different in New York than they were in Nebraska. Everyone seemed
in such a hurry in New York. No one was very friendly in Emily's school. Emily and her
brother, Ned, did not like their new community. They wished their dad would get transferred
back to Nebraska.

6. _____

It opened Friday with folk dancing from around the world. All day Saturday and Sunday
different countries exhibited their crafts and cooking. On Saturday night songs from all over
the world were sung by the International Singers. There was a huge fireworks display at
the festival's close Sunday night.

Topic Sentences

- Write a topic sentence for each of the following subjects. It should have enough content to be interesting and yet not reveal everything at once. "Answer" some of the "question" words and use descriptive words, too.

  Example: Frightened person: The frightened boy hid under the stairs.
  The frightened boy sat frozen in his hiding place under the stairs.
  Which one do you think is the better topic sentence?
  Why?

1. A special interest/hobby: _____

   _____

2. Eating at home: _____

   _____

3. A bee sting: _____

   _____

4. Mysterious footsteps: _____

   _____

5. Loud music: _____

   _____

6. Cool clothes: _____

   _____

7. Uproarious laughter: _____

   _____

8. Least favorite thing: _____

   _____

Support Sentences

- Topic sentences often introduce a thought, subject, or event.
  They should be backed up by one or more **support sentences**.
    Example: The frightened boy sat frozen in his hiding place under the stairs.
      He watched as the prowler flashed his light around the room.

The second sentence, a support sentence, tells more about the first sentence.

Rewrite the eight topic sentences you wrote from the previous page. Write a support sentence for each one.

1. _____

_____

2. _____

_____

3. _____

_____

4. _____

_____

5. _____

_____

6. _____

_____

7. _____

_____

8. _____

_____

Putting a Paragraph Together

Support sentences tell about the main idea expressed in the topic sentence. They support the topic sentence, and they support each other. Sentences that work together form a **paragraph**.

Read each topic sentence below. Write as many support sentences after it as it takes to answer the questions above each topic sentence. Write them in good order.

Questions: How do you know there are dogs available?
What kind are available?
What do you have to do to get one?

There are many dogs waiting to be adopted at the pound. _____

_____

_____

_____

_____

_____

Questions: Why is he on crutches?
Where and when did it happen?
How was Charlie treated?

Charlie will be on crutches for six weeks. _____

_____

_____

_____

_____

_____

Writing a Paragraph

Choose a topic from the box. Write the topic of your choice on the line below.

sister or brother
dogs as pets
after school responsibilities
the people next door
a mysterious package

_____

Write at least five facts about your topic.

_____

_____

_____

_____

_____

Look at what you have written. Do all the items relate to your topic? Add ideas if you think they are important. Number the items in an order that will make sense. Write a topic sentence about the topic you have selected. Follow the topic sentence with sentences that will support it. Let the list of items you wrote above help you write them.

_____

_____

_____

_____

_____

_____

_____

Look at what you have written. Is there a topic sentence? Do the sentences following support it? Is there an order to them? Is what you have written interesting? Are your thoughts clearly stated? Rewrite what you have written so the answers to these questions will all be YES. Be sure and check your punctuation.

Writing Instructions in Sequence

This house painter wants to paint the trim on the roof. However, she has a little problem— she left out an important step. What is it?

She forgot to bring the bucket of paint with her when she climbed the ladder.
In order to do anything—paint a house or brush your teeth—you have to perform a number of steps in the right **sequence**, or order.

Here is a list of steps for making papier-mâché. They are not in the correct sequence. Put them in the correct sequence on the lines below.

1. Dip the strips of newspaper into the mixture.

2. Apply the strips to the form.

3. Stir until the mixture is smooth, sticky, and wet.

4. Mix two parts water with one part flour.

First: _____

Next: _____

Third: _____

Finally: _____

Writing Instructions in Sequence

Write instructions for doing one of the following: blowing up a balloon; giving a dog a bath; making an ice-cream soda.

How to _____

First: _____

Next: _____

Third: _____

Finally: _____

Read the following instructions.

How Not to Paint the Floor

1. Begin painting at the doorway and work your way into the room.
2. Paint around the furniture that is too heavy to move.
3. After painting one third of the room, sweep and wash the rest of the floor.
4. After you've painted yourself into a corner, walk across the floor and leave the room.

Now rewrite these instructions. Tell how one should really go about painting a floor. Use **sequence words** like *first, next, then,* and *last*.

1. _____

2. _____

3. _____

   _____

4. _____

   _____

Writing a Direction Paragraph

A **paragraph** giving directions explains how to do something. Directions must be exact and in order.

Read the directions in the paragraph below and do what it tells you to do in the space to its right.

Draw a two inch square. Outside the upper left corner, write a **Q**. Outside the lower left corner, write an **F**. Outside the upper right corner, write a **D**. Outside the lower right corner, write a **T**. Draw a line from **D** to **F**. Draw a line from **T** to the **D-F** line. Make an **X** in the large triangle. Draw a face in the small triangle on the left. Color in the remaining triangle.

The directions above were given in an exact order. Sometimes directions use words that signal time like *first*, *next*, *now*, etc. Use the lines below to write a direction paragraph. Use words that signal time if you want. Give it to a friend to follow.

Writing a Descriptive Paragraph

A **descriptive paragraph** "paints" a picture in the reader's mind. Details help create a clearer picture.

After each of the following topic sentences, write details about what the sentences after them should describe.

The summer sun beat down on the big city's streets.

_____

The overturned flower vase on the desk was the first sign that the office was a mess.

_____

The old woman's face was parched from her years in the sun.

_____

The dachshund and the great dane were a funny sight walking down the street together.

_____

Choose one of the topic sentences from above. Rewrite it on the line below at the beginning of the paragraph. Write three or four sentences after it that will describe what you said they should. Let detail words and phrases help create a strong descriptive paragraph.

_____

_____

_____

_____

_____

Writing a Narrative Paragraph

A **narrative paragraph** tells about something that happened. The topic sentence should tell enough to make a reader want to read on. The sentences that follow the topic sentence are in the order in which they occurred.

After each of the following topic sentences, write a narrative paragraph using three or four sentences that show the order of events. Use your imagination to complete each paragraph.

On Sally's sixteenth birthday she got a car. _____

_____

_____

_____

A raccoon got into our garbage cans last night. _____

_____

_____

_____

Maggie crossed her fingers and shut her eyes when her father carried a large package

into the house. _____

_____

_____

_____

Writing an Opinion Paragraph

The topic sentence in a paragraph that expresses an opinion tells what the writer thinks or feels. The other sentences in the paragraph state the reasons for the writer's opinion.

Written at the start of each paragraph below is a topic sentence expressing an opinion. Pretend, if necessary, that you are in agreement with that opinion. Write three sentences after the topic sentence backing your belief.

Vegetables are good for everyone. _____

_____

_____

_____

_____

Studying with music produces the best results. _____

_____

_____

_____

_____

Living in Antarctica would not be a lot of fun. _____

_____

_____

_____

_____

Paragraph Building

Study this example to learn how to write a paragraph by answering the questions <u>who</u>, <u>where</u>, <u>when</u>, <u>how</u>, <u>what happened</u> or <u>what was done</u>.

TOPIC: A Class Trip

WHO: Mr. Thompson's and Miss Wilson's fourth grade classes went on a field

WHERE: trip. They went <u>to a huge industrial bakery on Lovett Street in Tylerville</u>.

WHEN: They left <u>on Thursday morning at nine o'clock</u>.

HOW: Some students <u>rode in cars</u> but most of the class <u>rode on the school bus</u>.

WHAT HAPPENED: When the group arrived at the bakery they were <u>greeted by their tour guides and shown each step used in baking bread</u>. At the end of the tour <u>each child received a small loaf of bread to take home</u>.

Write a paragraph about a class trip or family trip of your own. Answer these questions: who, where, when, how, what happened or what was done.

_____

_____

_____

_____

_____

_____

_____

Expanding Paragraphs

Rewrite the paragraphs below. Combine some of the sentences. Add adjectives. Change some of the verbs and nouns and add details to make them more specific. Change the order of words and sentences. Make the paragraphs more interesting.

The children walk home after school. They walk past the candy shop. They like candy. They want to buy candy. They go in and look around. They pool their money. They buy one candy bar. They cut it in six pieces. They eat it on their walk home.

_____

_____

_____

_____

Rex is my dog. He is a big dog. He is black and brown. He has long hair. He has black eyes. He has long ears. He likes to play. He does tricks. He is friendly. He is my friend.

_____

_____

_____

_____

My sister is a pest. She comes in my room. She takes my things. She follows me. She wants to do what I do. She tells Mother on me. She cries.

_____

_____

_____

_____

Expanding Paragraphs

Rewrite the paragraphs below. Use the material in each paragraph to create a better mental picture. Add details that will "paint" a mood or feeling and that will affect a reader's senses.

On summer nights my family sits on the porch after dinner. The fan blows air. My mom sometimes reads to us. Sometimes we talk or sing songs. Other times no one says a thing. We listen to the night. Summer nights with the family are nice.

_____

_____

_____

_____

_____

I smelled something when I came in the house. My mom was cooking dinner. She had made my favorite dessert. I went to my room to begin my homework. I could still smell Mom's cooking. When she called me for dinner I hurried to the table.

_____

_____

_____

_____

_____

Writing More Than One Paragraph

A paragraph is made up of sentences working together. Sometimes it takes more than one paragraph to tell something. Then paragraphs work together to tell about the main idea. Such writings have three parts. A beginning paragraph introduces what the composition is about. The middle part, which may be several paragraphs, backs up the main idea expressed in the introductory paragraph. The ending paragraph ties everything together. All of the paragraphs begin with topic sentences.

The main idea (**A**), the support, or middle, paragraphs (**B-D**), and the wrap-up (**E**) for **A Fourth of July Celebration** are written below. On a separate sheet of paper, jot down details you think might belong in each section. The details should answer the who, what, where, when, why, and how questions. Write at least three details.

A. The community was getting ready for the Fourth of July parade and picnic.

   1. _____
   2. _____
   3. _____

B. All the cars and bikes looked like American flags.

   1. _____
   2. _____
   3. _____

C. The Ladies' Club volunteered to make the food.
   1. _____
   2. _____
   3. _____

D. The firemen got the fireworks display ready to go.

   1. _____
   2. _____
   3. _____

E. The noon whistle signaled everyone to line up behind the band or to come stand along Main Street.

   1. _____
   2. _____
   3. _____

Using Notes in Writing Paragraphs

Write three paragraphs about what happens in the morning as you get ready for school. First make notes under the three topics listed below. Then write your paragraphs using your notes.

1. Who

_____

_____

_____

_____

2. What you do

_____

_____

_____

_____

3. What happens

_____

_____

_____

_____

_____

_____

_____

_____

_____

_____

_____

_____

_____

_____

_____

_____

Using Notes in Writing Paragraphs

A paragraph should be about one topic. First make brief notes about <u>bicycles</u> under the three topics listed below. Then write your paragraphs.

1. Description   2. Good points   3. Bad points

_____   _____   _____

_____   _____   _____

_____   _____   _____

_____   _____   _____

My bicycle is _____

_____

_____

_____

One good pooint about a bicycle is _____

_____

Another _____

_____

Some bad points about a bicycle _____

_____

_____

_____

Using Notes in Writing Paragraphs

One way to develop a paragraph is by using details. In order to do this an author must know about the topic.

In the exercises below, use encyclopedias, other reference books, and the Internet. First list details about the main idea as expressed in each topic sentence below. On another sheet of paper, rewrite each topic sentence as the first sentence in the paragraph. Follow it with three or four sentences that present details about the main idea expressed in the topic sentence.

The five Great Lakes are connected to each other by rivers or straits.

Details

_____

_____

_____

Paragraph

_____

_____

_____

Several American presidents have died in office.
Details

_____

_____

_____

Paragraph

_____

_____

_____

Combining Sentences

- A **compound sentence** is a sentence with two or more parts that are connected with a conjunction. Sentences that tell about the same person, place, or thing are easy to put together. When two words receive the same action of the verb, they can be combined into a compound object.

    Stacey likes math. Stacey likes art.

    Stacey likes **math and art**.

- A compound subject is two or more subjects that share a verb.

    Jill likes computers. Bob likes computers.

    Jill and Bob like computers.

If the subject that goes with the verb changes, be sure to check the verb form. In the first example above, the verb does not need to change. The subject is still just Stacey. In the second example, the subject is plural, so the verb must change. Verbs that go with plural subjects do not end in *s*.

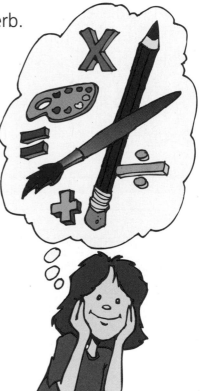

- If you create a sentence with **I** and another person, do not forget that **I** always goes last.

    I like music. Megan likes music.

    Megan and I like music.

Practice

Combine each pair of sentences into one compound sentence.

1. I like dogs. My dad likes dogs.

_____

2. My dad wants a beagle. I want a beagle.

_____

3. Pets need food. Pets need exercise.

_____

Combining Sentences

A **compound verb** has two or more verbs that share the same subject and are joined by a conjunction.

- Some sentences tell about someone or something doing different things. These sentences are easy to combine. Sometimes you can combine them with **and**.

    I went to the library. I checked out some books.
    I went to the library **and** checked out some books.

- Sometimes it makes more sense to combine the sentences with **but**.

    I wanted a mystery. I couldn't find one.
    I wanted a mystery **but** couldn't find one.

Practice

Combine each pair of sentences into one compound sentence.

1. Bats eat insects. Bats pollinate plants.

   _____

2. Bats hunt at night. Bats hide during the day.

   _____

3. Bats stay cooler at night. Bats don't worry about predators at night.

   _____

4. Some people are not afraid of bats. Some people put bat houses in their yards.

   _____

5. I will learn more about bats. I will know how to protect them.

   _____

Combining Sentences

- This is a basic sentence.
    The horse jumped.

- Often readers would like more information. They might
  wonder where the horse jumped or what it looked like.
  Here is some more information about the horse.
    The horse jumped. The horse was gray.
    It went over the fence.

- All of this information can be combined into
  one sentence.
    The gray horse jumped over the fence.

- Sometimes, when you combine sentences, you can get rid of details that are obvious.
  Here, there is no need to say the rider was on the horse.
    A rider was on the horse. She was skillful. She held on to the reins.
    The skillful rider held on to the reins.

There will usually be more than one way to combine sentences. Just make sure the
sentence makes sense.

Practice

Combine each pair of sentences into one compound sentence.

1. The robin was red. The robin made a nest. It was in a tree.

_____

2. The robin laid eggs. There were three. They were in the nest.

_____

3. Our cat was curious. He tried to climb up the big tree. The tree was in our yard.

_____

Combining Sentences

- Some sentences look almost exactly the same.
  I wanted yogurt. I wanted a muffin. I wanted cereal.

- Reading several similar sentences in a row like these can
  be boring. Try combining them into a series. If you name
  more than two things, put a comma after each one except
  the last one. Put **and** before the last one. Follow this rule
  even if you have more than three things.
  I wanted yogurt, a muffin**, and** cereal.

- Here is another example:
  I was tired. I was hungry. I was thirsty. I was grumpy.
  I was tired, hungry, thirsty**, and** grumpy.

- If you have just two items, you need **and**, but you do not need any commas.
  I wanted milk. I wanted orange juice.
  I wanted milk **and** orange juice.

Practice

Combine the groups of sentences into one sentence.

1. I invited Mario. I invited Ken. I invited Lee.

_____

2. We went skating. We played video games. We ate pizza.

_____

3. We talked about school. We talked about baseball. We talked about this summer.

_____

4. We helped Dad wash the dishes. We helped Dad clean the family room.

_____

Combining Sentences

- Some sentences can be combined using words such as *after, as, because, before, if, when,* and *while.*

    I was feeling ill. I went home from school early.

    I went home from school early **because** I was feeling ill.

A **clause** is a group of words that has a subject and a verb. In the sentence above, *I went home from school early* is a **main clause**. It can stand alone. *Because I was feeling ill* is a **dependent clause**. It cannot stand alone. Words like *because, when, after,* and *until* are used to introduce a dependent clause.

- Watch the order of the sentences you are combining. How you arrange them will affect their meaning. The following sentence has the same words as the sentence above, but it does not really mean the same thing.

    I was feeling ill **because** I went home from school early.

- If the dependent clause comes before the main clause, put a comma after the dependent clause.

    When I still felt ill the next day**,** I went to the doctor.

Practice

Combine each pair of sentences to make one sentence. Use the connecting words **because**, **when**, **after**, and **until**. Be sure to put the sentences together in an order that makes sense.

1. I opened the mailbox and saw a butterfly. I was surprised.

    _____

2. I forgot to get the mail out. I was watching the butterfly.

    _____

3. I watched the butterfly. It flew away.

    _____

4. It happened yesterday. I wrote about it in my journal.

    _____

Combining Sentences

- One way to make sure the reader understands how two sentences are related is to combine them using a dependent clause.

    Mark uses a wheelchair. No one expected him to play basketball.

    Because Mark uses a wheelchair, no one expected him to play basketball.

A **clause** is a group of words that has a subject and a verb. In the sentence above, *no one expected him to play basketball* is a **main clause** that can stand alone. *Because Mark uses a wheelchair* is a **dependent clause** that cannot stand alone.

- Words like *although, because, if, since, before, after, when,* and *even though* are used to introduce dependent clauses. Look at these examples. Notice that the two parts of the combined sentence are separated by a comma.

    When Mark challenged Rick to a game, Rick wasn't sure what to say.

    Because Mark was his friend, he said yes.

Practice

Rewrite each pair of sentences as one sentence. Start with the word in parentheses.

1. She is not the fastest runner. She is the most popular team member. (Although)

_____

2. She supports her teammates. She is fun to have at track meets. (Because)

_____

3. She loses a race. She shakes the winner's hand. (After)

_____

4. She has such a positive attitude. She deserves a blue ribbon! (Because)

_____

Combining Sentences

Practice combining the sentences below.

1. Harry climbed the oak tree.
   Nate climbed the oak tree.

   _____

2. The fifth grade played the teachers in soccer.
   The sixth grade played the teachers in soccer.

   _____

3. Cory cut strips of paper to make chains.
   Cory pasted strips of paper to make chains.

   _____

4. We saw the lion show at the zoo.
   We saw the monkey show at the zoo.

   _____

5. Mother bought a lot of food for the family party.
   Mother cooked a lot of food for the family party.

   _____

6. The children shivered when they got out of the cold water.
   The children shook when they got out of the cold water.

   _____

7. The scouts will sell lemonade to raise money.
   The scouts will sell cookies to raise money.

   _____

8. Our class studied about famous Americans.
   Our class wrote about famous Americans.

   _____

Combining Sentences

Continue to practice combining the sentences below.

1. My dad cut down the tree. My dad chopped it into logs.

   _____

2. The class washed cars on Saturday to raise money.
   The class waxed cars on Saturday to raise money.

   _____

3. Mom bought three chances for a dollar. Mom won one of the prizes.

   _____

4. The dog jumped on my bed. The dog woke me.

   _____

5. The girl scouts collect old papers. The boy scouts collect old papers.

   _____

6. Sarah prepared the potato salad. Sarah took it on the picnic.

   _____

7. We bought a sailboat. We sailed it on Saturday.

   _____

8. They nominated three candidates. They elected one of them class president.

   _____

9. They visited their cousins. They visited their grandparents.

   _____

10. We went to the movie. We bought popcorn and candy during the intermission.

   _____

Combining Sentences

- Some sentences include just one simple idea.
  I wanted some extra money. My mom said
  I couldn't have any more allowance.
  I decided to start a pet-care business. I asked
  my friend to be my partner.

To improve your writing, look for ways to combine
sentences to make your writing smoother.

- The sentences below probably do not sound right when they are read aloud.
  I wanted some extra money, my mom said I couldn't have any more allowance.
  I decided to start a pet-care business, I asked my friend to be my partner.

- To connect two sentences, you need more than just a comma. One way to
  connect them is to use words like *and, or, but,* or *so.*
  I wanted some extra money, **but** my mom said I couldn't have any more allowance.
  I decided to start a pet-care business, **so** I asked my friend to be my partner.

There is usually more than one way to combine sentences correctly.

Practice

Use commas and **and** or **but** to combine each pair of sentences below.

1. My mom really wanted me to take piano lessons. I didn't want to.

   _____

2. We decided I would take them for three months. Then we would talk about it again.

   _____

3. I hate to admit it. I really like playing the piano.

   _____

Combining Sentences

Change the two sentences to one sentence by using the word given.
The first one is done for you.

1. It snowed. I could use my new snowshoes.

   (because) __**I could use my snowshoes because it snowed.**__

2. We can play the game. The weather must be warm enough.

   (but) _____

3. The magician performed. The audience was spellbound.

   (when) _____

4. The children washed the windows. The grocer gave them money.

   (so) _____

5. Lois played the piano. Her brother played a flute solo.

   (while) _____

6. We jumped into the canoe. There were no paddles.

   (but) _____

7. Finish your lunch. Please clean your room.

   (after) _____

8. We went to the ball game. We ate lunch.

   (before) _____

9. She returned the sweater. It didn't fit.

   (since) _____

Combining Sentences

Sometimes several sentences can be combined. One sentence contains the main thought and each of the others adds only a word or two to the main sentence.

Combine the sentences in each group into one sentence. Add only the important words to the main sentence. The first one is done for you.

1. The dog ran down the street. The dog was barking. The street was crowded.

   The barking dog ran down the crowded street.

2. The snake went through the grass. The grass was tall. The snake was fast.

   _____

3. The girls baked a cake. It was a chocolate cake. There were three girls.

   _____

4. John finished the race. The race was two miles. He was first.

   _____

5. The boy brought his bike inside. His bike was damaged. The boy was unhappy.

   _____

6. Sara ate the treat. The treat was ice cream. She ate it quickly.

   _____

7. The birds sang songs. The birds were red. The songs were pretty.

   _____

8. Trees grow in the forest. They are elm trees. The forest is cool.

   _____

Friendly and Business Letters
Capitalization

- The street, city, state, and month are always capitalized in the heading.
  1415 **H**igh **S**treet
  Hometown, **VT** 02345
  March 8, 1998

- If you are writing a business letter, be sure to capitalize the person's title and name; the company's name if you include it; the names of the street and city, and state abbreviations. (Note: A list of state abbreviations appears on pg. 128.)
  Ms. **E**lizabeth **S**cott
  River **C**ity **P**ublishers
  4410 **M**ain **S**treet
  Greensville, **TX** 77701

- The greeting and the name are capitalized, as well as the first word of the closing.
  Dear **E**lizabeth,   **D**ear **M**s. **W**ilkins,   **S**incerely yours,

Practice

Read the friendly letter. Circle five words that should be capitalized.

210 Avondale street

Elmview, ny 08780

june 6, 2001

dear Fred,

I am a big fan of mystery books. Thanks for sending the books to me on my birthday. What would you like for your birthday?

your fan,

Esther Martinez

Friendly Letters
Punctuation

A friendly letter is a letter you write to someone you know well, like a friend or relative. It might be a thank-you note or just friendly news.

- A heading with a return address and the date is put in the upper right corner of your letter. That way, your reader will have your address and will know when you wrote your letter. Place a comma between the city and state abbreviations and between the date and the year.

  Bowling Green, OH   June 7, 2001

- The letter begins with the greeting and the name. Put a comma after the name.

  Dear Elise,

Next comes the body of the letter. This is whatever you want to say. When you are finished, you need a closing. Put a comma after the closing.

  Your friend,

Practice

Add four commas where they are needed in the letter below.

735 Brookhaven Drive

Antioch TN 77013

January 17 2000

Dear Aunt Mollie

   Thank you for sending me a T-shirt for my birthday. I'll wear it a lot. I hope you can come visit us soon. Maybe you can come to one of my violin recitals.

Love

Amber

Business Letters
Punctuation

A business letter is a formal letter you write to a company or to a person you do not know very well. The form and rules of punctuation used are different than those used when writing a friendly letter.

A comma goes after the date and city names in the heading and the inside address. A period goes after an abbreviation such as Mr. in the inside address and the greeting. The greeting is followed by a colon. Words and phrases such as Yours truly, Sincerely, or Best regards in the closing are followed by a comma.

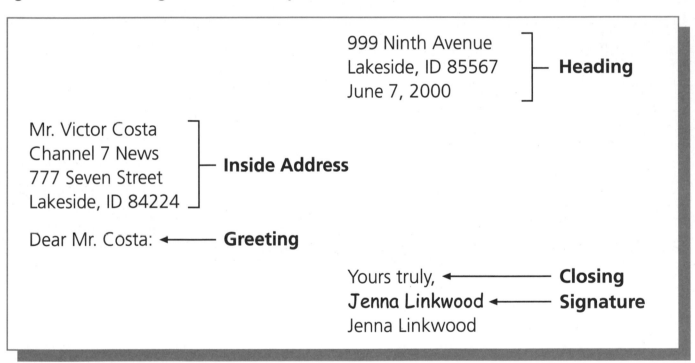

Practice

Add the correct punctuation to the heading, the inside address, and the greeting.

1. **Heading:**

   Foxwood Elementary School

   3498 Washington Street

   Creekville KS 71115

   April 17 2000

2. **Inside Address:**

   Ms Yolanda Moore

   Moore Bakery

   1212 Main Street

   Creekville KS 11115

3. **Greeting:**

   Dear Ms. Moore

Writing a Friendly Letter

Write a letter to a friend, thanking him or her for a gift you received on your birthday. Be sure to use good letter form and correct capitalization and punctuation.

Proofreading Practice:
Friendly Letter

Follow the directions below to show each part of a friendly letter.

Circle the:

Heading—orange   Greeting—green   Body—blue

Closing—yellow   Signature—purple

As you read the letter below, you will notice there are errors in capitalization and punctuation. Read the letter carefully. Use the proofreader's marks that you have learned to correct capitalization and insert commas where they are needed.

> 201 pioneer road
>
> trenton nj 21570
>
> june 5 2001
>
> dear ken griffey, jr.
>
>   You are my favorite baseball player. I admire your high batting average and get excited every time you hit a homerun. I'm sorry you were hurt during the '96 season and couldn't play for awhile.
>
>   My grandpa saw you play when you were just a little kid. It was at a father-son game when your dad ken griffey sr. played for the cincinnati reds. Grandpa said you looked like a natural athlete even then.
>
>   I am sending along one of your baseball cards. Could you please autograph it and send it back to me? I would really appreciate it.
>
>   your fan
>
>   richard e. anderson

Writing a Business Letter

Write a letter in response to the ad on the right. Tell why you are writing the letter. Tell about yourself and why you would be a good candidate for the job. Be sure to use good letter form and correct capitalization and punctuation.

Part-time summer work for student. Train on Job. Assist in Bike Shop. References. Write Joe Bickle, Box 56, Craig, CO 81625

Heading _____

_____

_____

Inside Address

_____

_____

_____

Greeting

_____:

Body

_____

_____

_____

_____

_____

_____

_____

Closing _____,

Signature _____

Proofreading Practice:
Business Letter

Follow the directions below to show each part of a business letter.

Circle the:

heading—purple	inside address—red	greeting—blue
body—green	closing—orange	signature—yellow

201 Valleyview Road

Phoenix, AZ 37715

August 24, 2001

Mr. Fix R. Upp, CEO

Lemon Motors Corp.

1000 Motorway Avenue

Detroit, MI 64718

Dear Mr. Fix R. Upp:

   I bought my 2001 Super Duper sports car in March of 2001 and have noticed several problems. Whenever I turn my parking lights on, the horn honks until I turn them off. My right turn signal makes the right window go down. Whenever I step on the brakes my radio blares full blast. I have never been able to get the car's trunk to open. I realize these are minor problems but they are driving me crazy! Please do something promptly.

Respectfully,

Mrs. Wanna Newcar

Addressing Envelopes:

Now that you have learned how to write a letter, you need to learn how to address an envelope. In the upper right corner of the envelope, write your name. Below your name, write your street address. The next line should include your city, state, and Zip code. In the center of the envelope, write the name of the person to whom you are writing. On the line below the person's name, write that person's street address followed by the person's city, state, and Zip code. Remember to capitalize the names of people and places. Also notice the comma placed between the city and state.

Dr. T. W. Smith
746 Lorain Lane
Chicago, IL 84417

Ms. Elizabeth Cornwell
P. O. Box 1945
770 Sunset Boulevard
Pasadena, CA 51012

Look at the envelope below. Correct the capitalization and punctuation. Use the envelope above to help you.

brad springer
500 juniper road
tampa fl 14158

brent g collins
3414 arlington drive
denver co 32717

Getting Started with the Writing Process

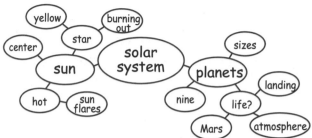

Suppose you want to write a paper on the solar system. Writing a paper can be done in these five steps in the writing process: **select**, **connect**, **draft**, **revise**, and **proofread**.

The first step is **selecting** a topic. Begin by narrowing the broad topic. Collect your ideas by writing **solar system** in a circle. Next, draw spokes around the center circle. At the end of each spoke, put a word in a smaller circle that comes to mind when you think of the solar system. Now think about each of the words in the smaller circles and do the same thing. You might come up with a cluster of words and ideas like the one above.

To further narrow your topic, look over the words in your cluster and choose one that interests you. Build another cluster around it. If you can't think of enough details, do some reading at the library or search the Internet.

The topic **Mars** would be an excellent selection. Repeat the process of clustering to get more details about this narrowed topic. **Connect**, or group, the ideas about the same thing by putting them together. As more ideas come to you, cluster them also. Writing is an ongoing process. Feel free to change things as you progress.

Now you're ready to write. **Draft** your ideas and details into paragraphs. Write about one cluster at a time. Next, **revise** the draft you wrote by deleting unnecessary information and rewriting what is not clear. Then, correct all mistakes in mechanics, usage, and grammar. Whenever possible, exchange drafts with a friend to **proofread** each other's writing because you tend to see what you *thought* you wrote in your own piece rather than what you actually wrote.

Tips for Your Own Writing:

- **Select** a topic that you find exciting.
- **Connect** ideas by clustering. Reading about the topic helps!
- **Draft** those clusters into paragraphs.
- **Revise** to make your writing as clear as possible.
- **Proofread** what is actually written on the paper, not what you thought you wrote.

Getting Ideas

You are your best source for ideas and questions when you get ready to write a paper. So draw on your experiences, opinions, and imagination. Trust yourself! What do you like best? Which experiences have you had that you remember most clearly? What do you care most about? Whom do you consider to be a hero or heroine? Make lists of those things. While you may not use all the ideas, you can save them for the next paper. Look at the lists and decide which topic is most appealing. Circle the topic that you would like to know more about or one that most interests you. One of those ideas will be your narrowed topic. Continue *brainstorming* or clustering around the narrowed topic for the details of your paper.

What if you need to find out about a topic you know nothing about? Don't panic! You know how to use the library. Get a general idea of the topic by going through books about it. Look carefully at the tables of contents. Review the topic in the encyclopedia. The Internet is also a great resource for information. Think about what you have read or learned from your reviewing. Ask yourself which details are most appealing to you. What would you like to know more about? The answer may be your narrowed topic. At this point, cluster your ideas to help determine some of the details. Connect, or group, those ideas that relate to each other. Remember, nothing is "written in stone." It can be changed. Writing is a process.

Now you're ready to write your first draft by using the details in the circles. Write about one connected group of details at a time. Write quickly and don't revise immediately; it might get in the way of your focus on your topic. Don't forget to be yourself!

Tips for Your Own Writing:

- Start with yourself and what interests you.
- Review your topic in the library, or on the Internet; however, once you have a general idea about your subject, go with what interests you.
- Cluster, cluster, cluster until you have enough ideas to start your first draft.
- Make adjustments as you progress; writing is a process.

Writing a Paragraph

A paragraph is a group of sentences that focuses on or develops a main idea. The main idea can be stated in one sentence. Other sentences in a paragraph give details that illustrate or support that main idea.

In the paragraph below, which sentence states the main idea? Which sentence should be deleted because it does not support the main idea?

Our Saint Bernard charged through the open doorway knocking over my two-year-old brother and an empty chair. Then the animal raced from the room kicking throw rugs out of its path as it went. My little brother also kicks the throw rugs all over the floors. Although we never saw our pet go into the kitchen, we did hear the wastebasket fall over. When we caught up with the beast, it was joyously bouncing around the living room, its tail fanning magazines to the floor. Although it never meant to do harm, our Saint Bernard was very destructive inside the house.

Does the first sentence state the main idea? No, the main idea is in the last sentence. To determine which sentence doesn't belong, think of the main idea. Which sentence does not relate to the dog being destructive in the house? If you decided it was the third sentence, you are absolutely correct.

Now notice how the paragraph is developed. The writer's description of the dog charging through the doorway takes the reader from one room to another. In other words, the writer arranged the details according to space, or spatial order, and also in time order.

Finally, determine if the paragraph is complete. To be complete, a paragraph must prove, answer, or support the main idea. Many good paragraphs also have a conclusion. Is everything that is necessary included in the paragraph above? Does it have a good conclusion? If you practice including all of the necessary ingredients in the paragraphs you write, you should become a successful communicator and writer!

Tips for Your Own Writing:

- Focus on or develop one main idea by relating the sentences to each other and to it.
- Follow some type of order in your supporting sentences.
- Read your paragraph to make sure everything that is necessary is in it, including a conclusion.

Staying on Topic

Staying on topic is easier in the writing process when you use clustering to narrow your subject. With the appropriate subject and an understanding of your purpose, you can write a well-crafted paragraph. State your main idea and how you feel about that main idea in your introductory or concluding sentence. You can state it in both if you wish. Just make sure you check each sentence in your paragraph to make sure it relates to or supports the main idea.

What else can help you stay on topic? Try to remember that whatever you write should state a main idea and purpose. Each paragraph in your piece should include details that illustrate or support the main idea. The order you use to organize these details depends upon the purpose of your writing. Be sure to delete any details that do not support the main idea. The end of a piece usually includes a closing sentence.

Now you be the judge. Does the paragraph below stay on topic? Can you determine the main idea? Do all the sentences support the main idea or should some of the sentences be deleted?

The score was tied with only three seconds left to play in the game. Chad stole the ball from our opponent just like he did in the game with Lincoln. The problem in the Lincoln game was that Blake, our best player, was out with a sprained ankle. We have never won a game without Blake. When Chad stole the ball, he was at the opposite end of the court. When he was about two-thirds up the floor, he shot the ball with both hands. The ball went into the basket, and we won the game!

Tips for Your Own Writing:

- Make sure your subject is narrow enough.
- Know your purpose for writing.
- Remember that writing should have a beginning, middle, and end.
- Determine if each sentence in the paragraph supports the main idea.

Proofreading Checklist

Every writer needs to proofread. Famous authors sometimes hire people to proofread for them. However, you'll have to do your own proofreading until you become famous. A proofreading checklist will help.

What is a proofreading checklist and how do you get one? Your teacher may give you a list of items to check when proofreading your writing at school. Otherwise, you can develop one yourself. Either way, spelling, capitalization, punctuation, usage, and grammar checks should be part of your list. You should also be sure your thoughts are clear, unified, and complete. Finally, you should include any specific mistakes that come up in your writing. You may have certain types of mistakes you tend to make over and over. Be sure these are on your checklist.

Do you need a proofreading checklist if you use a computer for writing? Yes! Computer programs can catch some mistakes but not all of them. For example, if you spell a word wrong, but you happen to spell another word that doesn't make sense in the sentence, computer spelling programs won't catch it. Read the paragraph below to see what happened when a computer spelling program didn't catch certain errors.

Righting stories it now hard to do. First, your save to chose some characters. When its time to thank of a plot. That problem will the people face? How will than solve this problem?

Here is what the writer meant to say:

Writing stories is not hard to do. First, you have to choose some characters. Then it's time to think of a plot. What problem will the people face? How will they solve this problem?

See the difference it makes when you proofread your work?

Tips for Your Own Writing:

Can your writing pass this test?
- All words are correctly spelled and capitalized.
- Each word in a sentence is used correctly, especially verbs and plurals.
- Sentences are properly punctuated.
- The meaning is clear, unified, and complete.

Narrative-Descriptive Story

A narrative is a story. You probably already know that because you have read stories or had them read to you most of your life. In a story, the writer wants to share with you some experience, either real or imagined. Each narrative has a **beginning**, **middle**, and **end**. The beginning often introduces the character or characters, the place, the time period, and the problem. The middle shows the characters trying to solve a problem or facing a crisis or conflict. The end resolves the main conflict, but endings to stories are not always happy ones.

Everyone likes to tell stories. Sometimes we tell stories about things that really happened. These stories, or narratives, usually tell about events in a chronological (time) order. The writer further develops the story by using detail to describe people, objects, or events. Those details are called **description.** Good description often appeals to the senses. The combination of time order and description helps the reader better understand and visualize a story.

The paragraph below, from the novel *The Jungle Book* by Rudyard Kipling, uses details to describe Rikki-tikki-tavi, an animal found by a young boy.

He was a mongoose, rather like a little cat in his fur and his tail, but quite like a weasel in his head and his habits. His eyes and the end of his restless nose were pink. He could scratch himself anywhere he pleased, with any leg, front or back, that he chose to use. He could fluff up his tail till it looked like a bottle brush. And his war cry, as he scuffled through the long grass, was "Rikk-tikk-tikki-tikki-tchk!"

Quite a picture, isn't it? It seems as though we not only see the mongoose, but we know him, too. What about your stories? Are your characters vividly described?

Tips for Your Own Writing:

- Make a story plan for your narrative that includes a beginning, a middle, and an end.
- Develop your story by using chronological order.
- Present your characters so that your reader knows them as well as you do.
- Use vivid description to develop characters and settings.

Expository Writing-Planning a Report

The purpose of an expository report is to give information about a subject using description, facts, or examples. That isn't a difficult task if you think in terms of steps. Just take one step at a time.

Step 1 involves finding a topic and narrowing it. Do that by writing down everything you know about a possible subject. Read about that subject in the library or do research on the Internet. Take notes and cluster ideas from those notes. Use the clustering to narrow your topic. For example, you might want to write about space exploration. That topic is too broad. How about "Apollo Missions" instead? Researching the subject, using a variety of resources, will not only help you develop a topic, but it will also let you know whether there is enough information about your topic to write a report.

Step 2 involves reading more about your subject and taking notes. An adult or a teacher may suggest that you use note cards. If so, write one fact or one detail on each card. Look at your notes, choose the fact that is most interesting to you, and use it as your main idea. All other facts and details can be used as main points to support that idea.

Step 3 involves determining which information that you have read fits with your main idea. If you used note cards, go through them and place all the cards that relate to the same point in the same stack. You will find that you may not use all your notes, and you may need to read some more and take more notes. Make sure each note supports your main idea. You may have three or four different stacks of cards indicating that you have three or four main points. Connecting your facts in this way helps organize your report.

Step 4 involves using your note cards to write your three or four main points in a list. Leave a space between each point. You are ready to use your stacks of note cards in the right order when you write your draft. If you did not take notes on cards, you will need to remember what you read about each of your three or four main points. When you begin writing, write an introduction to your whole topic. Then, write one section at a time. Add a conclusion. See the next page for more on writing your draft.

Tips for Your Own Writing:

- Choose a topic with at least three sources available for use.
- Gather information by reading and taking notes.
- Select the three or four main points for your report.
- Arrange your notes in a logical order and you are ready to start a draft.

Expository Writing-Writing a Report

If you followed the steps on the previous page and planned your report properly, the actual writing will be easier. Once you have selected your topic, narrowed it, and selected appropriate facts and details, you need to **draft** the information by putting it into paragraphs. Start by writing an introductory paragraph that tells what your report is about. Then, start the next paragraph with the first of the main ideas you listed. If you took notes or have note cards, read the ones that belong to that main idea and then write a paragraph or two on that subject. Do the same for each of the other main points. Then write a closing paragraph, or conclusion. It will summarize the points made in the body of the report. In the conclusion, leave your reader with some type of impression.

Revising is a step that is repeated as often as necessary. To revise, go through the report to rewrite sentences that may be vague or unclear. Also, check the report to see that all the sentences pertain to the main points. Delete any information that does not support or relate to the main idea. Verify that all the details and facts are arranged in a logical order. Add more facts and details if an area needs further development. Add charts, graphs, or illustrations if they would make the report more effective. Another revision strategy is to let an adult or friend read your report and suggest corrections, additions, or deletions.

A bibliography usually accompanies your report. A bibliography is a list of the books, magazines, and other materials you used to gather information. These are listed alphabetically. It is always the last page of a report. An adult or a teacher will let you know how to write your bibliography.

Now write your final copy. Add your bibliography and proofread everything before handing it in. Use a proofreading checklist. If necessary, rewrite the copy you thought would be your final copy!

Tips for Your Own Writing:

- Plan your report first.
- Use your list of three or four main points as a guide when you write.
- Write appropriate opening and closing paragraphs.
- Revise your report as many times as necessary.
- Proofread your report and ask an adult or friend to proofread it also.
- Write your final copy.

Writing a Persuasive Composition

Getting someone to believe something you believe or do something you want them to do involves persuasion. Persuasive writing convinces the reader of something. Before you begin to write a persuasive letter or piece of writing, you need to decide **what** you want to persuade someone to believe or do, and **who** you want to persuade.

An audience will not be persuaded unless you provide them with evidence or reasons to convince them. You will need to learn about your subject in order to make a convincing argument. Go to the library and check encyclopedias and almanacs for general information on your topic. Newspapers, pamphlets, and magazines will furnish you with evidence to prove your points. Books about your topic will provide you with even more evidence. The Internet can also be a source of information for you. List the reasons you find for your position.

Once your research has been completed, go through your list of reasons. Decide which of your points are the strongest and organize your reasons so that your strongest points are last. Saving your strongest evidence for the end of your paper will make a powerful impression on your audience. Number your list in the order that you want to present it.

Now write your draft. Start with a strong statement of your position on this topic and why you believe it. Then, present your reasons in their numbered order. Add any important information from your reading.

Next, revise your writing, eliminating unnecessary information and rewriting sentences that are not clear. Revise and rewrite as many times as you need. Proofread your paper for mechanical, usage, and grammar mistakes. Finally, write your final copy once you are convinced that your paper is complete and convincing.

Tips for Your Own Writing:

- Narrow your topic and identify your audience.
- Use the library and the Internet to research your topic and take good notes.
- Use your note cards to organize your points and write an outline.
- Write your first draft; then revise and proofread your persuasive letter or piece.

Postal State and Possession Abbreviations

Use these abbreviations on envelopes to be read by postal workers. In other writing, spell out the names of the states.

States

Alabama	AL
Alaska	AK
Arizona	AZ
Arkansas	AR
California	CA
Colorado	CO
Connecticut	CT
Delaware	DE
Florida	FL
Georgia	GA
Hawaii	HI
Idaho	ID
Illinois	IL
Indiana	IN
Iowa	IA
Kansas	KS
Kentucky	KY
Louisiana	LA
Maine	ME
Maryland	MD
Massachusetts	MA
Michigan	MI
Minnesota	MN
Mississippi	MS
Missouri	MO
Montana	MT
Nebraska	NE
Nevada	NV
New Hampshire	NH
New Jersey	NJ
New Mexico	NM
New York	NY
North Carolina	NC
North Dakota	ND
Ohio	OH
Oklahoma	OK
Oregon	OR
Pennsylvania	PA
Rhode Island	RI
South Carolina	SC
South Dakota	SD
Tennessee	TN
Texas	TX
Utah	UT
Vermont	VT
Virginia	VA
Washington	WA
West Virginia	WV
Wisconsin	WI
Wyoming	WY
District of Columbia	DC

U.S. Possessions

American Samoa	AS
Guam	GU
Puerto Rico	PR
Virgin Islands	VI

Capitalization
Sentences, People, Pets

- The first word in a sentence is capitalized.
  My best friend is named Marco.

- The names of people and pets are capitalized. Titles of respect such as **Miss**, **Mr.**, **Mrs.**, **Ms.**, and **Dr.** are capitalized. Do not capitalize doctor unless it is part of a name.
  Yesterday **M**arco let me walk **F**reckles, his new puppy.
  Freckles's veterinarian is **D**r. Williamson. He is a kind **d**octor.

- The pronoun **I** is capitalized.
  I've always wanted a puppy.

- The title of a relative is capitalized only if it is used as a name or part of a name.
  Marco's **f**ather offered to give me a puppy.
  I asked **M**other if I could have one.
  She said **F**ather and **U**ncle **J**ack are both allergic to dogs.

Practice

Read the paragraph below. Circle the five words that should begin with a capital letter. Draw a line through two letters that are capitalized and should not be.

> I wish you could meet (aunt) Rita. She's not really my ~~A~~unt, but since she's such a good friend of Mom's, I've always called her that. Aunt Rita works at a bakery, and whenever she visits, she brings me something different. (that's) not the only reason (i) like her. Aunt Rita is one of those people who makes you feel really important. (when) I told her I wanted to be a ~~D~~octor, she took me seriously. I'm pretty lucky to have a friend like Aunt (rita.)

7

Capitalization
Places, Holidays, Events

- The names of days, months, and holidays are capitalized. The names of the seasons are not capitalized.
  This summer, my father took me on a vacation. We left on a **T**uesday in **M**ay, right after **M**emorial **D**ay.

- Direction words are capitalized only when they name a region.
  We drove south from our home in the **N**ortheast.

- The names of places, buildings, and monuments are capitalized.
  In **W**ashington, **D.C.**, we saw the **L**incoln **M**emorial and the **W**hite **H**ouse.

- Important events are capitalized. Always capitalize the names of legislative bodies, such as the Congress, Senate, and House of Representatives.
  We also visited the memorial to the **V**ietnam **W**ar.
  The **S**enate was in session during our visit.

Practice

Read the sentences. Circle the ten words that should begin with a capital letter.

1. Mount (saint helens) is an active volcano.
2. It is part of the (cascade range.)
3. It is located in the southern part of (washington.)
4. The volcano erupted on (may) 18, 1980, killing more than 60 people.
5. In 1982, the (national volcano monument) was built there.
6. If you ever travel to the (northwest,) you should try to visit the monument.

8

Capitalization
Titles of Written Works

- Titles of books, magazines, movies, plays, stories, reports, poems, and songs are capitalized. Always capitalize the first and last word.
  *N*ational *G*eographic
  "*C*inderella"
  *J*ohnny *T*remain

- Articles (*a, an, the*) and short conjunctions (*but, and*) or prepositions (*of, to*) in titles are not capitalized unless they are the first or last words.
  *R*omeo and *J*uliet
  "The *B*attle *H*ymn of the *R*epublic"
  *J*ames and the *G*iant *P*each

Practice

The following titles are all in lowercase letters. Rewrite each title with the proper capitalization. If the title is in italics, underline it when you write it.

1. "every time i climb a tree" "Every Time I Climb a Tree"
2. "who has seen the wind?" "Who Has Seen the Wind?"
3. brutus the wonder poodle Brutus the Wonder Poodle
4. my buddy, the king My Buddy, the King
5. bridge to terabithia Bridge to Terabithia
6. the adventures of tom sawyer The Adventures of Tom Sawyer
7. "the gettysburg address" "The Gettysburg Address"
8. "puff the magic dragon" "Puff the Magic Dragon"

9

Proofreading Practice:
Capitalization

As you read the story below, you will notice that no words have been capitalized. Read the sentences carefully. Use the proofreader's mark (≡) to show which letters should be capitalized.

Christa McAuliffe

christa's interest in the space program began when she was a seventh-grade student and watched alan shephard, the united states' first astronaut, go into space. she was filled with excitement.

christa loved history. when she grew up she became a social studies teacher. when the opportunity arose for school teachers to apply for the next shuttle mission into space, christa was one of over 11,000 teachers who applied. imagine her exhilaration when she was the one chosen.

christa left her teaching position and her family behind in concord, new hampshire to train for her mission. her dream was coming true. she was planning to record every moment to show students that space travel could indeed be a part of their future.

then a terrible thing happened. the shuttle she was on, the *Challenger*, broke apart shortly after liftoff on january 28, 1986. christa and six other crew members lost their lives.

10

Punctuation
Commas in Series, Introductions, and Direct Address

- A comma is used to separate lists of items in a sentence. Place a comma after each item.
  My grandmother sent me to the store for tomatoes, lettuce, cucumbers, and celery.

- Some items on the list might have more than one word. Think of each group of words as an item.
  I'm always happy to do chores, run errands, or keep my grandmother company.

- A comma is also used after introductory words such as *yes*, *no*, and *well*.
  Well, I had lost the shopping list by the time I got to the store.

- If a speaker addresses someone by name, use a comma to separate the name from the rest of the sentence.
  "Thank you for going to the store for me, Tony."
  "Grandmother, wait to thank me until you see what I bought."

Practice

In the paragraph below, add eight commas where they are needed.

> Endangered species are animals that are in danger of becoming extinct. The cheetah, the Asian elephant, the snow leopard, and the spider monkey are all endangered animals. The animals living in lakes, rivers, or the ocean are harmed when humans produce water pollution. When land is cleared for houses or other uses, the animals who live there may die. Some animals are endangered because too many have been killed for their fur, tusks, bones, or other products used by people.

11

Punctuation
Commas with Introductory Phrases and Clauses

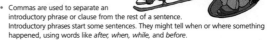

- Commas are used to separate an introductory phrase or clause from the rest of a sentence. Introductory phrases start some sentences. They might tell when or where something happened, using words like *after*, *when*, *while*, and *before*.
  After the snowfall, we put on our warm clothes and went to the hill behind our school.
  When we got to the school, Tricia and Suzanne were already there.

- Words like *although*, *if*, and *because* also start some sentences as part of a longer phrase or clause. The comma should follow the end of the phrase or clause.
  Although it was cold, we couldn't wait to start sailing down the hill.
  If you run and jump on your sled, it goes even faster.
  Because the hill was so steep, we kept tumbling off the sled at the bottom.

Practice

Add commas where they are needed in the paragraph below.

> When my grandmother was a young girl, she decided she wanted to be a doctor. Although almost all doctors were men at that time, she didn't let anything stop her. When she talked about her dream, nobody thought she was serious. If they had really known her, they would have believed her. While she was in college, she worked and saved every penny. After she graduated, she surprised everyone by going to medical school. Because she was so determined, her classmates respected her. Before she graduated, she had job offers from many hospitals. If you need a good doctor, I would recommend my grandmother.

12

Proofreading Practice:
Commas

You have learned that commas are used in sentences for several reasons. They are used

1. to separate a series of words or things.
   We had chicken, vegetables, and cake at the banquet.

2. to set off words of direct address.
   Richard, here is your hat.

3. to set off an introductory expression.
   Finally, I passed the test!

4. when two sentences are combined.
   Mary had a soda, and Tom had ice cream.

5. to set off appositives. (A word or phrase that explains a noun preceding it.)
   Fido, our neighbor's dog, takes our paper every morning.

As you read the sentences below, you will notice that commas are missing. Read the sentences carefully. Use the proofreader's mark (⋀) to show where commas should be added.

1. Laura, Emily, Jane, and Meghan met at the movies.
2. Sue Ellen, the Smith's daughter, goes to college in Columbus, Ohio.
3. My mom gave me a book, and Dad gave me a record.
4. Here, take this to the office.
5. We gave Miss Jones, our teacher, a going away gift.
6. The horse jumped over the fence, ran down the road, and hid in the barn.
7. Casey likes noodles, but he does not like spaghetti.
8. Christopher, come help me carry this box.
9. We went to our neighbors, the Mays, for dinner last night.
10. The team played Monday night, Tuesday afternoon, and last night.

13

Possessives
Singular and Plural Forms

If you want to show that something belongs to one person, you add an **-'s**.

- The hairdresser cut Susan's hair first.
  Then she styled Mrs. Harris's hair.

- If you want to show that something belongs to more than one person, add just an apostrophe (').
  All of the people in the shop know how to cut kids' hair.
  The two hairdressers' scissors made a snipping sound.

- You can follow the rules above to show that something belongs to a thing, too.
  All of the shop's seats were taken.

- Some words are already in the possessive form. You do not have to add anything to them. These words are my, your, his, her, its, our, and their. They are called possessive pronouns.
  Roberto got **his** hair cut.
  I decided to get **my** hair cut, too.

Practice

Rewrite each phrase using a possessive. The first one is done for you.

1. the dress that belongs to Katie — *Katie's dress*
2. the pet that belongs to all of the students — *the students' pet*
3. the shoes that belong to Marcus — *Marcus's shoes*
4. the car that belongs to him — *his car*
5. the toothbrush that belongs to me — *my toothbrush*
6. the cat that belongs to all of the girls — *the girls' cat*
7. the skates that belong to them — *their skates*

14

Possessives
Plural vs. Possessive Forms

- You usually add an **-s** or **-es** to make a noun plural.
  I have two excellent **friends**.

- You add **-'s** to show something belongs to someone.
  My friend **Julie's** favorite thing to do is go to movies.

- One mistake some writers make is to add an apostrophe (') when making a word plural. You do not need an apostrophe to make a word plural.
  My other **friend's** favorite thing to do is ride bikes.
  I like to do the things that both my **friends** like to do.

- You use an apostrophe to show that something belongs to someone or something.

Practice

Write the correct word in the blank. If you choose a word with an apostrophe, underline the word that names what belongs to the person or thing you wrote in the blank.

1. The _**clown's**_ <u>car</u> was very small and painted blue. (clowns, clown's)
2. The _**kids**_ all laughed as the clown tumbled out. (kids, kid's)
3. Then three more _**clowns**_ ran into the circus ring. (clowns, clown's)
4. The _**kids'**_ <u>eyes</u> grew as the clowns came into the stands. (kids, kids')
5. One clown gave two _**girls**_ some pop-up paper flowers. (girls, girl's)
6. Another clown took quarters out of two _**boys'**_ <u>ears</u>! (boys, boys')
7. A third clown held a ladder for three _**dogs**_ to climb. (dogs, dogs')
8. The _**dogs'**_ <u>collars</u> were big and ruffled. (dogs, dogs')
9. The fourth clown blew huge _**bubbles**_. (bubbles, bubble's)
10. The _**crowd's**_ <u>applause</u> filled the circus tent. (crowds, crowd's)

15

Proofreading Practice:
Possessives

As you read the article below, you will notice that apostrophes have not been added to show possessives. Read the sentences carefully. Use the proofreader's mark (ᵛ) to show where apostrophes need to be added. For extra practice, use the proofreader's mark (≡) to correct errors in capitalization.

Baseball's Beginnings

baseball may have developed from an old english sport of the 1600s called rounders. despite evidence of baseballs connection with rounders, some people believe baseball was invented in 1839 by a man named abner doubleday in cooperstown, new york. in an attempt to settle this argument, a special commission was appointed, and it came to the decision in 1907 that doubleday was indeed the inventor of the modern game.

alexander cartwright was the first to start a baseball club, the knickerbockers. Cartwrights written set of baseball rules made the game much like baseball today. early players received no money to play. in 1869, the cincinnati red stockings became baseballs first team to be paid, making them the first professional baseball team.

16

Contractions

- A **contraction** is two words written together as one word. One or more letters are taken out of the word to make it shorter. An apostrophe (') shows where the letter or letters are missing.

it is—**it's**	had not—**hadn't**
you are—**you're**	has not—**hasn't**
they are—**they're**	have not—**haven't**
cannot—**can't**	who is—**who's**
I will—**I'll**	you will—**you'll**
I would—**I'd**	could not—**couldn't**

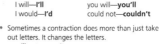

- Sometimes a contraction does more than just take out letters. It changes the letters.
  will not—**won't**

- Many contractions have **homophones**—words that sound like the contractions but have different meanings and spellings. Look at the homophones in these sentences:
  The kitten licked **its** fur. **It's** almost three months old.
  You're lucky to have a kitten. It likes to sleep in **your** bed.

- Contractions are used in informal writing or in stories to show how someone speaks. You probably should not use contractions in a business letter or a formal essay or report.

Practice

Write a contraction for the underlined words in each sentence.

1. I <u>cannot</u> go with you to the movies. _**can't**_
2. My mom <u>will not</u> let me go. _**won't**_
3. She said <u>it is</u> too late to go out. _**it's**_
4. Besides, I <u>have not</u> done my homework yet. _**haven't**_
5. Now I wish I <u>had not</u> watched TV after school. _**hadn't**_

17

Proofreading Practice:
Contractions

As you read the journal entry below, you will notice that no contractions have been used. Read the sentences carefully. Write the correct contraction above each underlined word pair.

Space Camp

Blast-off to space camp! <u>I am</u> [I'm] off to a city in the southwestern United States. I will be there for a whole month. I <u>could not</u> [couldn't] sleep well last night because I was so excited.

<u>We will</u> [We'll] spend the first week in buildings which have chambers that simulate feelings in space. One of the buildings contains an anti-gravity chamber.

The second week <u>we will</u> [we'll] sit behind mock control panels to learn what all of the buttons, dials, and levers do.

During the third week <u>we will</u> [we'll] each be fitted for a space suit and will learn how to use all of its features. Then <u>we will</u> [we'll] be taught how to eat and drink in space.

Week four will be the most exciting time of all. We step into the space camp shuttle for the first time and take a mock flight into space. <u>We will</u> [We'll] use all that <u>we have</u> [we've] learned during the month for our journey to the stars.

18

Homophones
New/Knew, No/Know,
Here/Hear, Right/Write, There/Their

The following pairs of words are **homophones**. Homophones are words that sound alike but are spelled differently and have different meanings. After you read the definitions, fill in each blank with the correct word.

- **New** means "recently come into existence or the opposite of old."
  Knew is the past tense of the verb know, which means "to be certain of something; be aware of."

    It was the first day of my ___new___ paper route.

    I ___knew___ it would be a good day.

- **No** means "not so; the opposite of yes." **Know** means "to be certain of something; to be aware of."

    Oh, ___no___, I thought.

    I ___know___ I broke Ms. Jackson's window when I threw the newspaper.

- **Here** means "in this place." **Hear** means "to listen to something."

    I couldn't ___hear___ anyone.

    I knocked on the door and said, "Is anybody ___here___?"

- **Right** means "correct." It can also mean a direction, as in your "right hand."
  Write means "to put down something on paper."

    I decided to ___write___ a note to Ms. Jackson.

    I knew that would be the ___right___ thing to do.

- **There** means "in or at that place; to or toward." **Their** is a possessive pronoun "belonging to them."

    I will go ___there___ and leave a note for the Jacksons.

    I hope they won't be too upset when they find out ___their___ window is broken.

19

Proofreading Practice:
Homophones

As you read the journal entry below, you will notice that some of the words have been used incorrectly. Read the sentences carefully. Use the proofreader's mark (⸜) to show which words should be deleted. Write the correct words above them.

The Right Combination

    It was the first day at my ~~knew~~ *new* school. I was a little apprehensive. I had all ~~knew~~ *new* supplies in my backpack: spiral notebooks, pens, pencils, ruler, protractor, and calculator. I located my locker on the second floor. ~~Their~~ *There* was a shiny, new combination lock on it. Other kids were opening ~~there~~ *their* lockers and putting jackets and supplies away. It occurred to me that I did not ~~no~~ *know* the combination of my lock. How did they all know theirs? Should I ask, or would they laugh at me? The bell would ring soon. I couldn't be late for class on the first day. As I stood ~~their~~ *there*, kids went by and said hello to me. Then they kept asking me when my birthday was. I thought that was a strange question. Why were they asking about my birthday? Wait a minute! I held the combination lock in my hand and tried the numbers of my birth date 10-28-86. Presto! I found the ~~write~~ *right* number. My locker opened. My day was saved.

20

Articles

A, **an**, and **the** are articles. They are words that are used before a noun.

- **The** is called a definite article. It is used to let your reader know you are talking about something definite, or specific.
    I went to see **the movie** that everyone is talking about.

- **A** and **an** are indefinite articles. Use them to let your reader know that the noun does not refer to anything or anyone specific.
    I wanted to buy **a snack**, but everything was too expensive!
    Next time I go to **a movie**, I'll eat before I go.

- When the noun you are using begins with a consonant or a vowel that sounds like a consonant, you use **a**. In *one*, *o* sounds like *w*.

a one-story house	a sidewalk	a library
a book	a boy	a hero

- When the noun begins with a vowel (a, e, i, o, u) or sounds like it does, you use **an**. In *hour*, the *h* is silent, so you use **an** with it.

an hour	an octopus	an apple
an owl	an elephant	an honor

Practice

Underline the correct article in each set of parentheses.

    I made (a, <u>the</u>) new friend today. He lives down (a, <u>the</u>) street from me. He was riding his bike on (a, <u>the</u>) sidewalk in front of my house. He asked if he could have (<u>a</u>, an) drink of water from our hose. He told me he moved here because his mom got (<u>a</u>, an) new job. She is (a, <u>an</u>) architect. That means she designs houses. He will go to (a, <u>the</u>) same school as I do. He's coming back to have dinner with us in (a, <u>an</u>) hour.

21

Proofreading Practice:
Articles

As you read the article below, you will notice that some articles have been used incorrectly. Read the sentences carefully. Circle the articles that are incorrect. Then write the correct articles above the words you circled.

Twisters

    Tornadoes, commonly called twisters, happen all over the world, but most occur in ⓐ *the* United States. Usually 700 or more form each year in the U.S.

    A twister is ⓐan *a* funnel cloud. In the Northern Hemisphere, twisters rotate counterclockwise. In the Southern Hemisphere, they rotate clockwise.

    A tornado forms when a warm air mass is pushed upward very quickly by ⓐan *a* colder air mass. Then more warm air rushes in and starts to twist. The twisting warm winds suck even more warm air into the center of the cloud. The twisting grows more powerful until ⓐan *a* funnel is formed.

    Not all funnels touch the ground. When twisters do touch the earth's surface, the violent rotating winds can demolish almost everything in their path. ⓐA *The* spinning winds can reach speeds of more than 200 miles per hour.

    The best protection against ⓐan tornado is to take cover in a basement. If a basement is not available, crouching in a bathtub or under ⓒthe sturdy piece of furniture away from windows is advised.

22

Recognizing Sentences

A sentence is a group of words that tells a whole idea.

* Look at the word groups below.

1	**2**
Kristie walked	Robin ran
3	**4**
crawled outside	Robin at the store

Write answers to the questions below.

1. Which word groups—1, 2, 3, and/or 4—would you say are complete sentences?
   1 and 2

2. Which word groups are not complete sentences?   3 and 4

3. What are the subjects in word groups 1 and 2?
   Kristie   Robin

4. What are the verbs in word groups 1 and 2?
   walked   ran

5. Does word group 3 contain a subject?   no

6. Does word group 4 contain a verb?   no

Think about how you answered the questions above. What two parts must a complete sentence have?

   subject   verb

23

Recognizing Sentences

Read the following word groups. Write an *S* next to each complete sentence. Write an *N* next to each word group that is not a complete sentence.

1. Hazel cooks   S
2. Walter the desk   N
3. The orange, red, and yellow flame   N
4. He walked quietly down the hill   S
5. Looking carefully through   N
6. The rain fell   S
7. Going to the fair   N
8. Lois jumped, and I yelled   S
9. He and the rhinoceros   N
10. The greatest day   N

A sentence begins with a capital letter and ends with a period, an exclamation point, or a question mark. Study these sentences.

Bruce nodded his head⊙   His eyes slowly. **closed**   **he** soon was asleep.

The sentences above have been proofread. As you have learned, *proofreading* means reading over what has been written and making corrections. Notice how the corrections above were made.

Proofread and correct the sentences below.

The cook stirred the mixture. then he poured it into a baking dish⊙
He **put** it into the oven. When do think it will be ready?

24

Completing Sentences

A sentence needs a good ending. Read the beginning of each sentence below. Write an ending to complete each sentence. Draw a picture of your complete sentence.

1. They won the important game with _____
   _____
   _____
   _____

2. We wanted it to snow so _____
   _____

   Answers and pictures will vary.

3. The sky _____
   _____
   _____

4. The smiling faces of the circus clowns turned to frowns when _____
   _____
   _____
   _____

25

Completing Sentences

A sentence needs a good ending. Read the ending of each sentence below. Write a beginning to complete each sentence. Draw a picture of your complete sentence.

1. _____
   _____
   _____
   and ants soon found the food.

2. _____

   becau

   Answers and pictures will vary.

3. _____
   _____
   and suddenly I found myself falling.

4. _____
   _____
   and then my alarm clock rang.

26

Writing Sentences

Look at each word. Write two words that tell something about the picture. Use the picture name and the two words to write a sentence about the picture.

1. ring

_____   _____

_____

_____

2. woman

_____   _____

_____

_____

3. mailman

_____   _____

_____

_____

4. socks

_____   _____

_____

_____

5. lizard

_____   _____

_____

_____

Answers will vary.

27

Types of Sentences
Statements, Questions, Exclamations, and Commands

- A statement is a sentence that simply gives information. It ends with a period.
  My teacher is Mr. Gonzales**.**

- A question asks for information; often begins with the words *who, what, when, where, why,* or *how*; and ends with a question mark.
  Who is Mr. Gonzales**?**

- Some statements sound like questions. Sentences that start with phrases like **I** *wonder* are usually not questions.
  I wonder who Mr. Gonzales is**.**

- An exclamation is a sentence that expresses a strong emotion, like fear, anger, or surprise. It ends with an exclamation point.
  You'll never guess where I saw Mr. Gonzales**!**

- A command is a sentence that asks someone to think or believe something. It can end with a period or with an exclamation point if you want to make it stronger.
  Tell me where you saw him**.** Quick, tell me**!**

- Using a variety of sentences makes it more interesting for your reader. You, as a writer, need to decide when to use each kind of sentence.

Practice

Next to each sentence, write its type: statement, question, exclamation, or command.

1. Have you ever met my friend Tina? _____**question**_____

2. She is a wonderful person. _____**statement**_____

3. I can't say enough nice things about her! ____**exclamation**____

4. Name one person who doesn't like her. _____**command**_____

5. Call her today! _____**command**_____

28

Statements from Questions

Write a statement in response to each question about you. Make sure each statement is a complete sentence.

1. What is your name? _____

2. When were you born? _____

3. Where were you born? _____

4. How much did you weigh? _____

5. How tall are you now? _____

6. What is your address? _____

7. What is the name of at least _____

8. Wh_____g? _____

9. What d_____have for breakfast today? _____

10. What do you usually do after dinner? _____

11. What hobbies or interests do you have? _____

12. Write a question about yourself. _____
Answer it. _____

Answers will vary.

29

Writing Different Types of Sentences

Use **only** the words in each box to write one of the four kinds of sentences. Use as many words in each sentence as you can. Some sentences will use more words than others. Some words may be used more than once, but not in the same sentence. However, all words must be used. Use correct punctuation.

Example:

in	where	pen	open	the	put	dog
don't	lives	live	does	his		

STATEMENT: _____

QUESTION: _____

COMMAND: _____

EXCLAMATION: _____

mon_			will	five	hundred	to
	tickets	sell	school	make		

STATEMENT: _____

QUESTION: _____

COMMAND: _____

EXCLAMATION: _____

out	switch	the	is	by	watch	for
where	lights	stand	the	on		

STATEMENT: _____

QUESTION: _____

COMMAND: _____

EXCLAMATION: _____

Answers will vary.

30

Sentence Diary

Talk to your friends and family members. Write the complete sentences that you hear. Write the name of the speaker who used each sentence.

STATEMENTS   SPEAKER

_____   _____

_____   _____

QUESTIONS

_____   _____

_____   _____

COMMA

_____   _____

_____   _____

EXCLAMATIONS

_____   _____

_____   _____

_____   _____

Answers will vary.

31

Proofreading Practice:
Sentence Types

As you read the story below, you will notice that no punctuation has been used. Read the sentences carefully. Insert periods, question marks, and exclamation points where they are needed.

Sandwich Saga

How did the sandwich get its name? In the early 1700s, a British nobleman called the Earl of Sandwich was playing cards with his friends. He was hungry but he didn't want to stop playing. He asked his servant to bring him a slice of meat between two pieces of bread. Although bread and meat must have been eaten this way many times before, the Earl's eating the food this way made it fashionable and gave it a name. The name "sandwich" caught on quickly and the sandwich's popularity spread.

Today there are many kinds of sandwiches. Some are served in long buns, such as hoagies, subs, or footlong hotdogs. Others are stacked vertically, like double-decker hamburgers, triple-decker club sandwiches, or dagwoods. Some are even served in pocket bread, also called pita bread. All of these and many more varieties share the name sandwich thanks to the Earl of Sandwich. What an amazing story!

32

Writing with Your Senses

A photographer can appeal to only one sense—sight. A good writer, however, through imagination, appeals to all the senses—**sight**, **hearing**, **smell**, **taste**, and **touch**.

Imagine that you are alone in the basement of an old house. The batteries of your flashlight have just gone dead. It is so dark that you cannot even see your own hand in front of your face. You must feel your way, step by step, through the dark basement, up the stairs, and out. What do you touch? Does anything brush against you? On the lines that follow, describe in detail four things that you feel as you try to get out of the house.

As you walk throu_____. Is it the wind or maybe an insect? Us_____ might hear in an empty house. Describe four sou_____m.

Answers will vary.

33

Writing with Your Senses

Eventually you reach a door and escape outside. What sounds do you hear now? List four sounds you might hear outside the empty house.

_____

_____

After your adventure in the house, you are frightened and tired. M____ you are hungry. You head right for home and raid the refrigerator. _____ follow, tell what you ate and how it tasted.

Answers will vary.

Write on Your Own

The sense of smell is the hardest sense to write about. Many people are not very aware of smells. Also, there aren't too many words to describe smells. Yet smell can change your mood—it can bring back memories, make you think of spring, or make you hungry. Take a walk in your imagination through your house or neighborhood. What smells do you remember? How would you describe them? On another sheet of paper, write a list of at least ten things your nose remembers. Then describe them in complete sentences.

34

Identifying Nouns

A noun is a word that tells who or what did the action or was acted upon by the verb in the sentence. *Book, school, desk, kids, teacher,* and *room* are all nouns, and each has a form to show plural, or more than one. People's names are nouns, too.

- One way to improve your writing is to be sure you have chosen just the right noun. Nouns tell your readers exactly what the sentence is about. Compare these sentences. I saw a **thing** in the sky. I saw a **meteor** in the sky.

- When you write, you should think about how you can make your nouns more specific. Say *gentleman* instead of *person* or *toddler* instead of *kid*, for example.

Practice

Circle the nouns in this paragraph.

Have you ever heard (people) say they saw a shooting (star?) (Stars) don't really shoot across the (sky.) "Shooting (stars)" are (meteors.) A (meteor) can be made up of (rock) or other (materials.) It becomes brighter when it comes into the (atmosphere) (a (layer) of (gas) surrounding (Earth.) (Meteors) are like (fireworks) when they come into the (sky.) Most (meteors) turn to (dust) by the (time) they get to (Earth.) But if the (meteor) doesn't, it is called a (meteorite.) The largest known (meteorite) on (Earth) is in (Africa.) It weighs 55 (tons.) Another (meteorite) made a (crater) in (Canada) more than 2 (miles) in (diameter.)

35

Identifying Nouns

Practice

Look at this sentence: **I saw something** ~~...write some nouns~~ you could use instead of "somet~~hing"~~

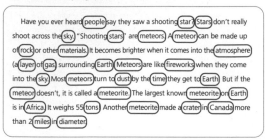

Sentences will vary.

Revise

Sample answers given.

Read the paragraph. Write a more specific noun above each underlined noun.

> Thursday
> Thanksgiving is my favorite <u>day</u> of the year. Early in the day, my sister and I
> plates
> set the table. We put <u>things</u> at each place. Then we arrange <u>decorations</u> for a
> flowers
> kitchen   turkey Relatives
> centerpiece. Mom is busy in the <u>room</u> preparing the <u>food</u>. <u>People</u> arrive just
> cards
> before three o'clock. After dinner, we play <u>games</u>. We end the celebration with
> pie
> a big helping of Grandma's special <u>dessert</u>!

36

Writing More Exact Nouns

What's wrong with the ad below?

Well, a boat can be a beautiful new ocean liner or a dumpy old rowboat. Before you pay five hundred dollars, you'd probably want to know exactly what kind of boat you'd be traveling on. A more **exact noun**, like rowboat, gives more infor~~mation~~ than a general noun, like boat.

Read the following sentences. Replace each unde~~rlined noun with~~ an exact noun on the lines. You can use your own ~~...~~ ~~li~~st below.

Saint Bernard ~~...~~
fruit sal~~...~~   daisies

Answers will vary.

1. The ~~...~~ ~~ke~~eping her warm during the snowstorm.

2. The fiel~~d...~~ ~~cov~~ered with <u>flowers</u>. _____

37

Writing More Exact Nouns
(Continued)

3. That <u>food</u> tasted good. _____
4. Suddenly a <u>sound</u> rang out in the night. _____
5. Ted drove up in his new <u>vehicle</u>. _____

For every general noun below, write two more exact nouns. The first one has been done for you.

1. animal   kangaroo   robin
2. clothes   _____   _____
3. furniture   _____   _____
4. snack   _____   _____
5. feeling   _____   _____

Rewrite the ~~...~~ ~~u~~nderlined noun or noun phrase with a more ~~...~~

Answers will vary.

> The ~~two guy~~s went hiking one day. <u>One guy</u> walked into <u>this place</u> and saw <u>this thing</u> peering through the trees. They just stared at each other for <u>some time</u>. <u>The other guy</u> dropped his <u>stuff</u> and took off. <u>The first guy</u> jumped and screamed, and <u>another person came</u> and scared it away.

38

Writing More Exact Nouns

Read the sentences. Look at the underlined nouns. Use more exact nouns to rewrite the sentences to make them more interesting. The first one is done for you.

1. The <u>bird</u> sang in the tree.

   The cardinal sang in the tree.

2. The <u>animal</u> built a nest.

   _____

3. The <u>people</u> roller skated in the park.

   _____

4. The <u>lady</u> baked cookies for th~~_____~~

   _____

5. The ~~_____~~ own.

6. The <u>mar~~____~~</u> the food promptly.

   _____

7. The <u>flowers</u> grew right outside my bedroom window.

   _____

8. The <u>tree</u> blew over in the storm.

   _____

9. The <u>person</u> broke his arm.

   _____

Answers will vary.

39

Identifying Pronouns

Pronouns can be handy. They take the place of a noun, so you can say *he, she, it, they, her, him, them,* and so on without naming the same person, place, thing, or idea over and over again. But be careful! If you use pronouns too much, your reader might be confused.

- Read the sentence below. What is the problem with the use of the pronoun *she*?
  When Mom talked to Beckie today, she was angry.

- In this example, it is not clear who was angry, Mom or Beckie. One way to fix the problem is to replace *she* with the noun.
  When Mom talked to Beckie today, **Mom** was angry.

- Another way to fix the problem is to rearrange the words.
  Mom was angry when she talked to Beckie today.

Practice

Rewrite each sentence so that it is clear to whom or what the underlined pronoun refers. **Suggested answers given.**

1. Dad and Jack invited <u>his</u> cousins to visit.

   Dad and Jack invited (Dad's or Jack's) cousin to visit.

2. When Latrice and J. J. got there, <u>she</u> was tired.

   When Latrice and J.J. got there, (Latrice or J.J.) was tired.

3. We offered them lemonade, juice, or soda. They said they wanted some of <u>that</u>.

   They said they wanted some (juice or soda or lemonade).

4. When our friends came, I asked Dad and Jack if <u>they</u> wanted some lunch.

   When our friends came, I asked Dad and Jack if our friends wanted some lunch.

40

Identifying Pronouns

Practice

~~paragraph~~ about a hobby that you share or sport ~~____~~ with a group of friends. Tell something about each of ~~____~~ds. Do not use any pronouns. Circle words that can be replaced with pronouns.

_____

_____

Re~~____~~

Write a ~~____~~ above each underlined word or phrase.

People ~~____~~r the world are trying to find more sources of energy that will
They
reduce ~~____~~ <u>People</u> are also trying to conserve fossil fuels by using renewable
He
resources. ~~____~~ Owen Fisher uses solar panels to heat his home in Arizona. <u>Owen</u> has
They
installed solar panels on the roof to collect the sun's rays. <u>The sun's rays</u> are then
converted directly into electricity. Amanda Perez has several windmills on her
She
Nebraska farm. <u>Amanda</u> uses the wind's energy to generate electricity. Tom and
Cathy Clark change the energy in a waterfall into electricity to run their mill in
them
northern Maine. This source of natural power has saved <u>the Clarks</u> thousands of
it
dollars. Water power is a clean, reusable source of energy, but <u>water power</u> often
requires the construction of costly dams. Some people use <u>geothermal energy</u> to
heat buildings. Geothermal energy comes from the hot, molten rock in Earth's core.

41

Identifying Adjectives

An adjective is a word that describes a noun or a pronoun. *Kind, generous,* and *helpful* are all adjectives that describe friend in the example above. An adjective is a word that usually can fit in both these blanks:
The _____ tree is very _____.

Adjectives give readers more information about a subject. There is a big difference between a *kind friend* and a *fake friend.*

- Adjectives usually come before the words they describe.
  a **funny** friend   a **happy** friend

- Like nouns and verbs, adjectives work best when they are specific. Which adjective in the sentences below tells you more about Maria?
  Maria is **nice**.   Maria is **generous**.

When you write, try to use adjectives that give the reader a clear idea.

Practice

Underline the nineteen adjectives in the paragraph.

I peered out my window into the <u>dark</u>, <u>deserted</u> street. A <u>pale</u>, <u>yellow</u> streetlight cast a <u>fuzzy</u> glow onto the sidewalk. A policeman, with a <u>shiny</u> badge pinned to his <u>navy</u>, <u>blue</u> uniform, made his <u>usual</u> rounds. Our <u>friendly</u> neighbor, on his way to his <u>demanding</u> job, dashed out of the building and let the <u>heavy</u> door slam behind him. <u>A jet-black</u> cat sped across the sidewalk and into the darkness. I looked again at the <u>crescent</u> moon and got into my bed. Just as I was about to pull my <u>soft</u>, <u>warm</u>, <u>faded</u> quilt over my <u>tired</u> body, I heard a <u>faint</u> sound.

42

Identifying Adjectives

Practice

Write the next paragraph of the story on the previous page. What do you think this person heard? Use at least six adjectives that show what it looked like, sounded like, moved like, maybe even smelled like.

_____
_____
_____
_____
_____
_____

Revise
Sample answers given.

Write a more interesting adjective above each underlined adjective.

> beautiful   delicious
> It was a nice day in July. We packed a good lunch and bicycled over to Sunnyhill
>   crisp   Colorful
> Beach. We could hardly wait to jump into the cool water. Some umbrellas dotted
>   Hyper   bouncing
> the sand. Nervous mothers and moving toddlers lined the water's edge. The
> eager   huge   compact
> happy swimmers raced out to the big raft. Several small sailboats circled the lake.
>   wonderful
> It was a great day!

43

Writing More Exact Adjectives

The man in the picture just sold you a radio that doesn't work. You want to warn your friends. How would you describe the man? Jot down a few ____ the following lines.

_____

Answers will vary.

You probably know that describing him as "some guy" won't help. You want to use more exact adjectives so your friends can picture him clearly in their minds. Try to use **exact adjectives** whenever you write a description.

Look at the pair of adjectives in each of the following sentences. Underline the more specific adjective.

1. The man had a (rasping, funny) voice.

2. He had a (weird, dangerous) look in his eye.

3. The man's jacket was (crumpled, old looking).

4. His movements were (strange, jerky).

5. His (choppy, peculiar) manner of speaking made me feel (nervous, bad).

44

Writing More Exact Adjectives

Read the paragraph. It's about the farmhouse in the picture below.

> It was a nice, old farmhouse built over a pretty brook. Next to the house was
> a lovely meadow with fantastic flowers everywhere. The house was a wonderful
> building with neat little windows and doors.

We know from the sample paragraph that the writer liked the farmhouse, but we don't know what the farmhouse looked like. Rewrite the paragraph on the lines below. Look at the picture and choose exact adjectives that describe what you see.

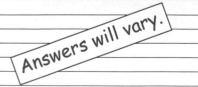

Answers will vary.

45

Identifying Adverbs

- An **adverb** is a word that describes a verb, adjective, or even another adverb. This adverb describes the adjective *long*.
  It was a **very** long book.

- Like adjectives, adverbs give your reader more information. Adverbs usually tell *how* something is done. They often end in -ly, as in *quickly, quietly,* and *happily*.
  Steve chose his book **carefully**.

- Adverbs can often be placed in several different places in a sentence. This adverb describes the verb *finished*.
  Steve **quickly finished** his book.
  Quickly, Steve **finished** his book.
  Steve **finished** his book **quickly**.

- Some writers use the adverb *very* too much. When a word is used too often, it loses its meaning for your reader. Look at these other words to use or other ways to say *very*.
  Steve is **very** smart.   Steve is extremely smart.
  He reads **very** much.   He is an avid reader.

- Many writers confuse the adverb well with the adjective *good*. Here they are used correctly.
  Steve is a **good** student.   (an adjective describing **student**)
  He does **well** in school.   (an adverb telling **how**)

Practice
Sample answers given.

Complete each sentence with an adverb that best fits in the sentence.

> The teacher ____quickly____ passed back the papers. Eric wasn't doing very
> ____well____ in the class. He ____cautiously____ looked at his paper. He
> ____happily____ showed his A paper to his friend.

46

Identifying Adverbs

Practice

Fill in each blank with an adverb of your own.
Suggested answers given.

Trish was taking her dog Beast for a walk. Something black and white

ambled ___lazily___ out from under the bushes. Beast stopped and began
                    1

to growl ___loudly___. Trish took one look and ___quickly___ ran back
                 2   3

to the house. Beast ___slowly___ walked home. Trish ___carefully___ led
                          4   5

Beast out into the yard and sprayed him off with the garden hose. She

___sternly___ scolded her pet, "Beast, you must ___quickly___ learn to
        6   7

stay away from skunks!"

Revise

Add an adverb to each sentence. Remember that adverbs can often be placed in several different places in a sentence.

            lovingly
Example: The mother cat licked her baby.   **Sample answers given.**
                         ^

        heatedly   slowly
The wind and the sun were discussing who was stronger. A traveler walked
                      ^   ^
                                            quickly
down the road. The sun said, "Whoever can make the traveler remove his cloak
                                      hard   ^
will be the stronger one." The wind began to blow on the traveler. The traveler
                           ^
       tightly   soon   brightly
wrapped his cloak around himself. The wind gave up. The sun shone. The
           ^   ^   ^
  eventually   grudgingly
traveler found it too hot to wear his cloak. The wind had to admit that the sun
        ^   ^
was the stronger one.

47

Writing More Exact Adverbs

- **Adverbs** tell how, when, or where something happens.
  Gino is singing <u>loudly</u> <u>in the shower</u> <u>now.</u>

- An adverb can be a single word, such as *loudly* or *now*.
  Many adverbs are formed from adjectives by adding *ly*:
  loud loud<u>ly</u>   fond fond<u>ly</u>   slow slow<u>ly</u>

- A **phrase**, or group of words, can also act like an adverb. These **adverbial phrases** begin with **prepositions**. For example, the adverbial phrase *in the shower* begins with the preposition *in*. Here are some other adverbial phrases:
  He left <u>at midnight</u>.   She hid <u>under the bed</u>.   I walked <u>with speed</u>.

Complete the following sentences by writing an adverb or an adverbial phrase which answers the question in parentheses.

1. I told my brother I'd go to the museum _____

2. That knight's armor is standing _____

3. I like the way it ch_____
                            (how?)

4. I see _____
              (where?)

5. I don't m_____ being with my little brother, he usually acts _____
                                                                (how?)

6. We will go to the library _____
                        (when?)

Answers will vary.

48

Writing More Exact Adverbs

- You can use adverbs to answer more than one question in a sentence. For example:
  Joanna was swimming. (*Where* and *when* was she swimming?)
  Joanna was swimming underwater at three o'clock.

- You can also vary the position of the adverbs in a sentence. For example:
  At three o'clock, Joanna was swimming underwater.

Rewrite each of the following sentences on the lines below. Add an adverb that answers the question in parentheses.

1. Oscar plays the trombone. (How and where does he play it?)

_____

2. Mr. Lopez found the _____

_____

3. The dog _____ared! (How and when did it disappear?)

Answers will vary.

49

Verbs
Regular and Irregular

- A **verb** is a word that tells about something that happens. To make a verb tell about something that happened in the past, you usually add *-ed*.
  We **walk** to the park.   We **walked** to the park.

- If the verb ends in *e*, you don't need another *e*. just add a *-d*.
  We **share** popcorn.   We **shared** popcorn.

- If the verb ends in *y*, you usually change the *y* to an *i* and add *-ed*.
  We **carry** our lunch.   We **carried** our lunch.

- Many verbs do not follow these rules. They are irregular.

- Most irregular verbs would not sound right if you tried to add *-ed*.
  We **run** up the grassy hill.   We **ran** up the grassy hill.
  We **eat** our lunch.   We **ate** our lunch.

- Here are some irregular verbs in the present and past tense:

Present	Past	Present	Past	Present	Past
buy	bought	fall	fell	is	was
do	did	find	found	see	saw
draw	drew	get	got	sit	sat
drink	drank	give	gave	stand	stood
drive	drove	go	went	write	wrote

Practice

Write the correct past-tense verb above each underlined verb.
       sat   drew
1. I <u>sit</u> under a tree at the park.   3. I <u>draw</u> pictures of the children.
     watched   tried
2. I <u>watch</u> children playing basketball. 4. I <u>try</u> to make each picture perfect.

50

Verbs
Regular and Irregular

Proofread

There are ten mistakes in forming the past tense in this paragraph. Use the proofreader's mark (⌿) to delete each incorrect verb and write the correct verb above it.

Example: They ~~gived~~ me a ticket to the concert.
gave

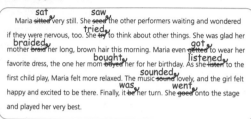

    sat   saw
Maria ~~sitted~~ very still. She ~~seed~~ the other performers waiting and wondered
          tried
if they were nervous, too. She ~~try~~ to think about other things. She was glad her
braided
mother ~~braid~~ her long, brown hair this morning. Maria even ~~getted~~ to wear her
         got
      bought   listened
favorite dress, the one her mom ~~buyed~~ her for her birthday. As she ~~listen~~ to the
          sounded
first child play, Maria felt more relaxed. The music ~~sound~~ lovely, and the girl felt
      was   went
happy and excited to be there. Finally, it ~~be~~ her turn. She ~~goed~~ onto the stage
and played her very best.

Write On Your Own

On a separate sheet of paper, write five sentences that tell about something that has already happened. You may choose to write about a family trip, a day you spent with a friend, or you may choose your own idea. Remember to put the verbs in the past tense.

51

Verbs
Using Past-Tense Forms

On the line in each sentence that follows, write the past tense of the verb in parentheses. Use your dictionary to check on irregular forms if you need help.

1. Alicia and I (try) __tried__ to move the piano the other day.
2. We accidentally (break) __broke__ an expensive lamp.
3. Alicia (scrape) __scraped__ the paint off the wall and (rip) __ripped__ the carpet.
4. I (trip) __tripped__ and (sprain) __sprained__ my ankle.
5. The piano leg (fall) __fell__ through the floor.
6. The noise (bother) __bothered__ my uncle, who was sleeping in the room below.
7. He (dream) __dreamed__ that he was on a ship.
8. He (think) __thought__ that an iceberg hit the ship.
9. So he (grab) __grabbed__ a pillow and (jump) __jumped__ overboard.
10. He (awake) __awoke__ on the floor.

52

Verbs
Using Past-Tense Forms

- Look at the underlined verbs in the following sentences.
  Dad <u>has worked</u> for the city for twenty years.
  I <u>have sampled</u> all thirty-two flavors of ice cream.

- Notice that *has* and *have* are followed by forms of verbs that look like the past tense (*worked, sampled*). For regular verbs, the form following *have* is the same as the past-tense form. But many irregular verbs have different forms after *have*. Here are a few. You will find others listed in your dictionary.

Verb	Past	Form After <u>Have</u>
come	came	come
eat	ate	eaten
go	went	gone
ring	rang	rung

Write in the correct past-tense form of the verb in parentheses for each sentence below. Use a dictionary if you need help.

1. Bjorn has __brought__ you a present. (bring)
2. Aunt May has __made__ your favorite cake. (make)
3. Have you __seen__ it yet? (see)
4. Why haven't you __told__ me about it? (tell)
5. The ball has __broken__ the window. (break)
6. Susie has __decided__ to try out for the class play. (decide)
7. What has Chita __hidden__ under the bed? (hide)
8. Have you or your sister __flown__ on an airplane? (fly)

53

Verbs
Subject-Verb Agreement

- Every sentence has a subject and a verb. Present-tense verbs have two forms: the **plain form**, like *play*, and the **s form**, like *plays*. The verb form must go with, or agree with, the subject. Look at these examples.

  Gloria <u>plays</u> softball.   The girls <u>play</u> softball.
  She <u>plays</u> softball.   I <u>play</u> softball.
  Gloria and Juan <u>play</u> softball.   You <u>play</u> softball.
  They <u>play</u> softball.   We <u>play</u> softball.

Use the sentences above to help you complete the following generalizations.

1. When the subject is a singular noun or the pronoun *it, she,* or *he,* use the __s form__ form of the verb.

2. When the subject is a plural noun, two nouns joined by *and,* or the pronoun *I, you, we,* or *they,* use the __plain form__ form of the verb.

To make the *s* form of most verbs, you add *s* or *es*. Some verbs change form slightly.
do   do<u>es</u>   bury   bur<u>ies</u>   have   h<u>as</u>

Underline the correct form of the present-tense verb in the following sentences.

1. Every day I (<u>jog</u>, jogs) along the river.
2. My sister (run, <u>runs</u>) five miles before school.
3. She (go, <u>goes</u>) around the park five times.
4. My two spaniels (<u>scurry</u>, scurries) next to me most of the way.
5. Then they (<u>take</u>, takes) off after a cat or a bicycle.
6. Two police officers always (<u>pass</u>, passes) us.
7. They (<u>smile</u>, smiles) and (<u>wave</u>, waves) at us.

54

Verbs
Subject-Verb Agreement

- The word **be** has some special present-tense forms:
  - I am singing. You are singing. He is singing.
  - We are singing. The girls are singing. They are singing.

Fill in the blank with the correct present-tense form of **be**.

1. I __am__ going to the movies tonight.
2. Tom __is__ coming with me.
3. We __are__ taking the bus downtown.
4. Philip and Chris __are__ meeting us there.
5. Terry, you __are__ welcome to come, too.

Write On Your Own

Write a short diary entry for your favorite TV or book character. Tell what you think she or he might be doing or thinking now. Use present-tense verb forms. Underline each verb form you use.

55

Verbs
Subject-Verb Agreement

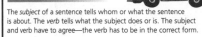

Review:

The *subject* of a sentence tells whom or what the sentence is about. The *verb* tells what the subject does or is. The subject and verb have to agree—the verb has to be in the correct form.

- If the subject is a singular noun, or *he, she,* or *it,* add *-s* to the verb.
  The bus **comes** through our neighborhood.
  It usually **runs** on time.
- If the subject is a plural noun, or *I, we, you,* or *they,* do not add *-s* to the verb.
  Many kids **walk** to school.
  I **walk** to school every day.
  We all **walk** together.
- If the verb ends in *o, sh, ch,* or *s,* add *-es* instead of *-s.*
  Ricky **wishes** he could ride his bike to school.
  I **do**, too. He **does** a lot of complaining.
- If the verb ends in *y,* change the *y* to *i* and add *-es.*
  I **try** to convince my mom that it would be okay.
  He **tries**, too, but she thinks we should go together.
- There are some common verbs that do not follow these rules.
  I **have** we **have** he **has**
  I **am** we **are** he **is**

Practice

Fill in each blank with a present-tense verb that agrees with the subject.

1. (to eat) She __eats__.
2. (to bring) He __brings__.
3. (to talk) Rosa __talks__.
4. (to be) Susan __is__.
5. (to fall) It __falls__.
6. (to like) He __likes__.

56

Verbs
Subject-Verb Agreement

Proofread

There are seven errors in subject-verb agreement in this paragraph. Use the proofreader's mark (ℊ) to delete each incorrect word and write the correct word above it.

Example: My sister and I ~~keeps~~ keep the same schedule.

After school every day, my sister and I walk home together. Our mom ~~call~~ calls us from work to make sure we are home and safe. I finish my homework and help my sister while she ~~do~~ does her homework. Then we have a snack. I make the snack, and my sister ~~clean~~ cleans the dishes. My mom usually ~~leave~~ leaves a list of chores for us to do after our homework is done. Every Monday my sister ~~fold~~ folds laundry and I ~~helps~~ help her put it away. We're always glad when my mom ~~get~~ gets home from work!

Practice

Write five sentences telling what members of your family do to help out in your home. What chores do you do? What do other family members do?

Sentences will vary.

57

Verbs
Subject-Verb Agreement

- When the subject is first and the verb comes right after it, it is easy to be sure the verb is in the right form.
  I like to go to the rodeo.
  Terry likes to go, too.
- The subject is not always followed by the verb. No matter where the verb is, you still need to make it agree with the subject. Notice that in these examples, the verb comes *before* the subject.
  Have you ever been to the rodeo?
  Has your cousin ever been invited to come, too?
- Sometimes the subject and verb are separated by a phrase that gives more information about the subject.
  My cousin from Dallas always **comes** to see the rodeo.

When you are revising, look at every verb and its subject, wherever it is. Be sure they agree.

Practice

The subject and verb in each sentence are underlined. Rewrite each sentence so that the subject and verb agree.

1. Has you ever looked through a telescope?
   Have you ever looked through a telescope?
2. The telescope in Rosa's apartment are powerful.
   The telescope in Rosa's apartment is powerful.
3. The stars in the sky sparkles like diamonds.
   The stars in the sky sparkle like diamonds.
4. I wonder what an astronaut traveling through space see.
   I wonder what an astronaut traveling through space sees.

58

Verbs
Subject-Verb Agreement

Practice

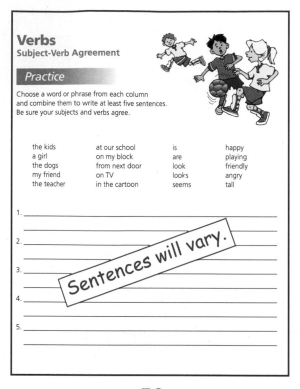

Choose a word or phrase from each column and combine them to write at least five sentences. Be sure your subjects and verbs agree.

the kids	at our school	is	happy
a girl	on my block	are	playing
the dogs	from next door	look	friendly
my friend	on TV	looks	angry
the teacher	in the cartoon	seems	tall

1. _____
_____
2. _____
3. _____
4. _____
5. _____

Sentences will vary.

59

Proofreading Practice:
Subject-Verb Agreement

As you read the article below, you will notice that there are errors in subject-verb agreement. Read the sentences carefully. Use the proofreader's mark (℘) to delete the incorrect verbs. Then write the correct verbs above them.

The Origin of Football

American football ~~develop~~ *developed* from the game of soccer. In many foreign countries, soccer ~~are~~ *is* called football. Football was first played in the eastern part of the United States in the mid-1800s. It was mostly a kicking game. The primary way goals ~~was~~ *were* scored was to kick the ball over the opponent's goal line. Often thirty players ~~plays~~ *played* on a team at once.

Over the years, many of the rules ~~changes~~ *changed*. Some rules were intended to help the teams score in other ways, like carrying the ball over the goal line. Running, tackling, and blocking ~~was~~ *were* the main elements of football in the 1900s. The forward pass became popular around 1913 and ~~adds~~ *added* excitement to the game. It also helped to eliminate some of the injuries caused from the tackling brawls of early football. Today football ~~are~~ *is* one of the most popular sports in America.

60

Writing More Exact Verbs

Review:

- A verb tells what the person, place, idea, or thing in a sentence is doing, or it links or connects the subject to the rest of the sentence. A verb might tell about being rather than acting, as in this sentence.
  The sun **is** hot.

- Compare the verbs in these two sentences below. Which verb gives you a better picture of what happened?
  The plate **fell** to the floor.
  The plate **crashed** to the floor.

Crashed is a better choice for this sentence because it tells the reader exactly how the plate fell—with a crash!

When you write, decide exactly what you want your reader to know. Then choose your verbs carefully to get your message across.

Practice

Underline the verb in each sentence. In the space after each sentence, write a word from the word bank that could replace the verb to make the sentence more powerful.

scribbled	gazed	announced	flip
leaped	blasted	slammed	sped

1. She <u>hit</u> the ball out of the park. **slammed**
2. His bike <u>went</u> down the hill. **sped**
3. <u>Turn</u> over the pancake. **flip**
4. She <u>jumped</u> over the fence. **leaped**
5. He <u>looked</u> at the trophy. **gazed**
6. She <u>played</u> her radio. **blasted**
7. He <u>said</u> his name. **announced**
8. He <u>wrote</u> a note. **scribbled**

61

Writing More Exact Verbs

Practice

Write three simple sentences to tell something that happened today. For example, you might write: I got out of bed. I ate breakfast. I walked to school.

<u>Sentences will vary.</u>
_____
_____

Choose two or three verbs from your sentences. Write them in the column on the left. On the right, write your ideas for more powerful verbs. Can you think of a verb that tells how something was done? What else do you want your reader to know?

First-draft verbs   **Better verbs**
<u>Answers will vary.</u>   _____
_____   _____
_____   _____

Revise

Suggested answers given.

Write a more exact verb above the underlined word(s) to improve the paragraph.

Just before I <u>got on</u> the plane, I <u>looked</u> up at the sky. It was full of dark, *boarded* *gazed* threatening clouds. I <u>put on</u> my seat belt and <u>held</u> the armrests as the plane took *buckled* *grabbed* off. I <u>looked</u> at the other passengers. No one else seemed nervous. Just then a *glanced* bolt of lightning <u>happened</u> right next to my window. The pilot <u>said</u> that our ride *flashed* *vowed* might be bumpy. I knew I should have taken the train!

62

Writing More Exact Verbs

A good writer chooses verbs carefully. To express an idea well, a writer should use an **exact verb**.

Think of one or more verbs that could be used instead of *walked* in the following sentence to express the ideas below. The first one has been done to get you started.

The girl <u>walked</u> down the street.

Sample answers given.

1. happiness   skipped, pranced
2. haste   sprinted, dashed
3. clumsiness   faltered, tripped
4. pain   limped, stumbled
5. tiredness   staggered, trudged

Write more exact verbs for the verb said in the following sentence to express the ideas below.

The boy <u>said</u>, "I did it."

1. loudness   shouted, yelled
2. sadness   cried, wimpered
3. softness   whispered, murmured
4. happiness   cheered, shouted
5. confusion   mumbled, muttered

63

Writing More Exact Verbs

Your writing will be more interesting and more accurate if you use one exact verb instead of a general verb helped by an adverb. For example:

Butch, Slim, and I <u>walked slowly</u> past Creely's dump.
Butch, Slim, and I <u>trudged</u> past Creely's dump.

Sample answers given.

Think of one exact verb to replace the underlined verb and adverb in the sentences below.

1. "Such a dull summer," Butch <u>said unhappily</u>.   grumbled
2. Just then Elly Moss's time machine <u>came noisily</u> into sight.   thundered
3. Its silver and glass discs <u>shone brightly</u> in the sun.   glittered
4. In a second we were <u>moving quickly</u> after it.   rushing
5. The time machine landed on the courthouse lawn; we were <u>looking carefully</u> at the cockpit.   peering
6. The cockpit slid open, and Elly Moss and a strange creature <u>came quickly</u> out of the machine.   jumped
7. "I'm just back from the twenty-third century," Elly <u>said loudly</u>, "and do I have news for you!"   shouted

64

Proofreading Practice:
Exact Verbs

As you read the report below, you will notice that some of the verbs are underlined. Read the sentences carefully. Replace each underlined verb with an exact, more interesting verb. For extra practice, use the proofreader's mark (≡) to correct the errors in capitalization.

Verb choices will vary.

Liberty Bell

          resides
Why is a bell that no longer rings so famous? The silent bell <u>is</u> in Liberty Bell

Pavilion in ₱hiladelphia, ₱ennsylvania. Many people come to view this symbol of liberty.

        became
       Before ₱ennsylvania <u>was</u> a state, the people living there had the <u>liberty bell</u>
constructed
<u>made</u> in ₱ngland and shipped to ₱hiladelphia. It was rung along with church bells
signal   cracked
to <u>tell</u> of the signing of the <u>declaration of independence</u>. It <u>broke</u> while it was

ringing but was soon fixed.

       For more than 80 years ₱hiladelphians rang it every <u>fourth of july</u>. Then it

cracked again when it was rung during the funeral of a famous judge, ⱼohn
                     preserved
ₘarshall. The bell was not repaired. It has never rung again, but it is <u>saved</u> as a

symbol of independence for all of the citizens of the <u>united states</u>.

65

Comparisons

When we **compare** things, we look for ways in which they are similar and ways in which they are different. One way to compare different things is to tell how they look, feel, sound, smell, or taste. We use **adjectives** to make such comparisons.

List the adjectives from the picture above.

bigger	colorful
greener	delicious

66

Comparisons

Notice that we change short adjectives that compare two items by adding **er** at the end. We use **more** in front of longer adjectives when we compare two items.

Write a sentence with an adjective to compare each pair below.

1. a baseball and a basketball: _____

2. a flower and a weed: _____

Sentences will vary.

3. a pencil and _____

- When we use adjectives to compare more than two items, we add **est** to short adjectives. We use the word **most** in front of longer adjectives.
  Of the three kittens, Snowball has the <u>whitest</u> fur.
  But Tiger is the <u>most playful</u> of the three.

Choose one of the groups below. Write three or more sentences using adjectives to compare the different members of the
an apple, a cherry, and a banana
a mouse, a dog, and an elephant
a skateboard, a bike, and a

Sentences will vary.

Write On Your Own

Think of two TV characters, two places, or two meals to compare. Choose one that you like a lot and one that you don't like. Then, on another sheet of paper, write five sentences comparing the two. Try to use an *er* or more adjective in each sentence in your paragraph.

67

Writing Comparisons Correctly

As you have learned, an adjective is a word that describes a noun, which is often a person, place, or thing.

- Sometimes you will want to compare two people, places, or things. You can usually do this by adding -er to the adjective that describes them.
  My uncle is **taller** than my dad.

- If there are more than two subjects, add -est to the adjective.
  My aunt is taller than both of her brothers. She is the **tallest**.

- With longer adjectives, it sounds better to use **more** and **most**.
  She is **more athletic** than Uncle Bob.
  She is the **most athletic** of all my relatives.

- The words **good** and **bad** are special words.
  You do not add -er and -est or use more or most.
  My dad's spaghetti sauce is **good**.
  His macaroni and cheese is **better**.
  His noodle soup is the **best**.

  My aunt's tuna casserole is **bad**.
  Her meat loaf is **worse**.
  Her green bean salad is the **worst**.

Practice

For each sentence, choose the correct word or phrase in the parentheses and write it in the blank.

1. This winter was the __coldest__ winter of the century. (coldest, most cold)

2. It snowed __ı́ɑ́der__ this year, too. (harder, more hard)

3. Grandfather said it was the __worst__ winter he had ever seen. (baddest, worst)

4. The __best__ thing about winter is the sledding. (best, goodest)

5. Th __most awesome__ l is right behind our house. (most awesome, awesomest)

68

Writing Comparisons Correctly

Proofread

This paragraph has five mistakes in adjectives that compare. Use the proofreader's mark (⸘) to delete the incorrect word or words and write the correct word or words above them.

Example: There are ~~badder~~ *worse* things than losing a race.

Mal Lin used to be the fastest runner in the whole neighborhood. One summer I grew an inch. I raced her and I was ~~more fast~~ *faster* than she was! She was angry with me. I got even ~~angrier~~ *angrier* than she was because she wouldn't admit I won. But then she apologized. She told everyone that I was the ~~most faster~~ *fastest* runner in the neighborhood. I'm glad we're friends again. We've been ~~goodest~~ *best* friends since we were five. It would be silly to let a thing like running spoil it. I think having a good friend is the ~~importantest~~ *most important* thing in the world.

Practice

Write four sentences comparing the people in the picture above.

Sentences will vary.

69

Proofreading Practice:
Comparisons

As you read the article below, you will notice that some of the adjectives used to compare have not been used correctly. Read the sentences carefully. Cross out the comparisons that are incorrect. Write the correct adjective above the words you circled.

Fun in the Sun

Florida could be called the "Funshine State" as well as the "Sunshine State." Many people vacation there, because of the warm, sunny climate and the many interesting things to do there.

Near the center of the state, in Orlando, Florida, families flock to theme parks, such as Walt Disney World and Sea World. On the west coast at Tampa is another park, Busch Gardens, which features exhibits of rare birds, African animals, and tropical plants. ~~More further~~ *Further* south is Florida's ~~most~~ largest lake, Lake Okeechobee, which covers about 680 square miles. The Everglades and Big Cypress Swamp spread over ~~mostest~~ *most* of southern Florida. Sports fans might want to visit Miami, the home of the Orange Bowl. At the extreme southern tip of Florida are the Florida Keys, made up of small islands which curve southwest for 150 miles. Key Largo is the ~~larger~~ *largest* of all these islands and is a popular vacation spot.

70

Writing Similes

- A **simile** is a comparison that uses the words **like** or **as**. These words clearly show that a comparison is being made.

  Anita's hair is **as** curly **as** lamb's wool.
  Cutting her hair was **like** shearing a sheep.

Find five similes in these lines from "A Visit from Saint Nicholas." Then on the lines below, write what is being compared in each simile.

> His eyes, how they twinkled! His dimples, how merry!
> His cheeks were like roses, his nose like a cherry!
> And the beard on his chin was as white as the snow;
> The stump of a pipe he held tight in his teeth,
> And the smoke it encircled his head like a wreath;
> He had a broad face and a little round belly,
> That shook when he laughed like a bowl full of jelly.
> —Clement Moore

Find five similes in these lines from "A Visit from Saint Nicholas." Then on the lines below, write what is being compared in each simile.

1. __cheeks__ are compared to __roses__
2. __nose__ is compared to __cherry__
3. __beard__ is compared to __snow__
4. __smoke__ is compared to __wreath__
5. __belly__ is compared to __jelly__

Similes can make our spoken and written language more colorful. Frequently similes are funny or descriptive. Here are two ways to say the same thing.

  He was very happy.
  He was as happy as a mosquito at a crowded beach.

71

Writing Similes

Complete the following similes. Try to think of fresh and different comparisons.

1. clumsy as _____
2. hot as _____
3. Your suit looks like _____
4. She plays tennis as if _____
5. as nervous as _____
6. a laugh like _____
7. He walks like _____

Now write similes that de_____ _____ ituations. Use the lines below.
the cafeteria d_____
waking up _____ ne last day of summer vacation

Answers will vary.

_____
_____
_____

Write On Your Own

The following poem is made up of similes.

> My grandmother was tall, like the sunflowers near the porch.
> Her eyes were gray, like the granite walls of the courthouse.
> My grandmother was strong, like the tree roots which push up sidewalks.

On another sheet of paper, write your own simile poem. First, think about someone or something you have strong feelings for—a member of your family, a friend, a pet, your home. Next, decide what you will compare the person or thing with. Finally, write your comparisons in a series of similes.

72

Writing Similes

- Sometimes to create a stronger mental picture, two unlike things are compared.

  The boy walked <u>slowly</u>. A turtle is <u>slow</u>.
  The boy walked like a turtle.

The boy and turtle are compared. Slowness is what they have in common. Comparisons such as these are called **similes**.

Read the sentences below. A word (or words) is underlined in each one. Think about that word and of what other thing that word might be characteristic. Rewrite the sentence and make a comparison using **like** or **as** to connect the two things. Be creative.

1. The wind blew **in a circle**. _____
2. The sly fox watched his next meal **quietly** from behind the rock.

   _____
3. The morning was **crisp** after the storm.

   _____
4. The road was **narrow and wind**_____

   Answers will vary.
5. Chad _____ ceive the award.

6. The sno_____ ntly on the roof.

   _____
7. Paper flew **up** around the room when the window was opened.

   _____
8. The boy was **mean** when he did not get what he wanted.

   _____

73

Writing Metaphors

- A **metaphor** compares two things without using like or as. A metaphor uses a word or phrase which means one thing to describe another.

  This classroom is a zoo.
  The ghost of a moon slipped behind the trees and disappeared.

Tell what two things are being compared in each metaphor above.

1. __classroom and zoo__

2. __ghost and moon__

Metaphors can help readers see things in new ways. Metaphors add color and imagination to writing.

Look at the pictures below. What do they remind you of? On the lines at the top of the next page, write a metaphor to describe each picture.

1.    2.

74

Writing Metaphors

1. _____

2. _____

What do the following things remind you of? Us[ing] [sent]ences about
four of the items on the lines below.

   a spring day   a di[ff]   an old, worn-out car
   a stingy person   an alarm clock

Answers will vary.

1. _____

2. _____

3. _____

4. _____

Write On Your Own

A metaphor can be just one sentence. Or a whole paragraph
can extend the metaphor and explain it. For example:

> Grace was a walking tape recorder. She was the nosiest person in the school.
> Her ears were microphones. She seemed to have a special sense that could pick
> up a piece of hot gossip at the other end of the cafeteria. She heard—and
> remembered—everything.

Choose one of the metaphors you wrote for above, or think of another. On a separate
sheet of paper, write a paragraph that extends and explains your metaphor.

75

Writing Metaphors

- Sometimes two things that are different, but have a
  characteristic in common, are compared to create a
  stronger mental image.
     The cook was a jewel.

The cook really was not a jewel, but he was so good that
he was valuable like a jewel. Like or as were not used in
this comparison. Such a comparison is called a **metaphor**.
Metaphors may replace various parts of speech.

Underline the metaphors in the following sentences. Write what each metaphor means.

1. The pillow <u>was a rock</u>.   The pillow was uncomfortable, not soft.
2. The <u>heat crashed</u> down on the highway workers.   It was extremely hot.
3. She walked with <u>lead in her shoes</u>.   She walked slowly.
4. Chris <u>was heartbroken</u> when Sissy told him good-bye.   Chris was very sad.

_____

Fill in the sentences with words from the box to create metaphors.

sandpaper	music to my ears	moaned
a rat's nest	eats tacks	cotton balls

1. Mr. Hubbard's cabinet under the sink was a rat's nest
2. The news is music to my ears
3. The mounds of snow were cotton balls
4. In the winter my hands are sandpaper
5. The elevator moaned at the end of a long day's work.
6. Mr. Howard eats tacks for breakfast.

76

Similes and Metaphors

Rewrite the following simple sentences to make them
more interesting or clearer. The first time, use adjectives
and adverbs. The second time, use a simile or metaphor.
You may need to rearrange some words.

1. The children cheered. _____

2. The sun blazed. _____

3. The geese honked. _____

4. The lions roared. _____

Answers will vary.

5. The _____

6. The w[ind] walked. _____

7. The man yelled. _____

8. The fish swam. _____

9. The radio blared. _____

10. The lamp glowed. _____

77

Polishing Your Writing

When you have finished writing, you should **proofread** your work to correct any
errors in capitalization, commas, end punctuation, apostrophes, verb forms, and so
on. You may also revise your work. To **revise** means to rewrite with improvements.
When you revise, you may choose more exact nouns, verbs, or adjectives. You may add
adverbial phrases. You may combine sentences to improve paragraph rhythm or to clarify
your meaning.

Read the paragraph below. Rewrite the sentences using more exact nouns, adjectives,
and adverbs. Be creative.

> The streets were crowded. They were narrow. We heard sounds filling the air.
> People went from store to store. Someone dropped a lot of packa[ges]. [Ma]ny people
> rushed over to help. We all felt good.

Answers will vary.

78

Polishing Your Writing

Revise the next paragraph yourself. Try to make each subject and verb exact. Use the tools you have learned to make the paragraph more interesting.

The car came down the street. It stopped. The man asked for directions. A woman was on the sidewalk. She had a dog. She told the ma___ng. He drove away.

Answers will vary.

79

Main Idea and Topic Sentences

Look at this picture.

What is the main idea of the picture? You might say that one fisherman caught a lot of fish but the other pulled up a rubber tire.

Paragraphs also have main ideas. The **main idea** of a paragraph is what the paragraph is all about. The **details** in the paragraph tell about the main idea.

Write a paragraph about the picture above. You already know the main idea. Add some details to complete your paragraph.

Answers will vary.

80

Main Idea and Topic Sentences

Sometimes the main idea is stated in one sentence. This sentence is called the topic sentence. The **topic sentence** can be found anywhere in a paragraph, but usually it comes at the beginning or end of the paragraph. Do you have a topic sentence in your paragraph that you wrote on the previous page? If so, underline it.

Read the following paragraph. Underline the topic sentence.

Either the well was very deep, or Alice fell very slowly, for she had plenty of time as she went down to look about her and to wonder what was going to happen next. First, she tried to look down and make out what she was coming to, but it was too dark to see anything. Then she looked at the sides of the well and noticed that they were filled with cupboards and bookshelves. She took down a jar from one of the shelves as she passed. It was labeled "ORANGE MARMALADE," but to her great disappointment it was empty. She did not like to drop the jar for fear of killing somebody underneath, so she managed to put it into one of the cupboards as she fell past it.

—Lewis Carroll

Write On Your Own

On another sheet of paper, write a paragraph about the strangest thing you have ever seen. Experiment with where you place the topic sentence. Write the paragraph in three different ways. First, begin with the topic sentence. Next, end with the topic sentence. Finally, rewrite the paragraph with the topic sentence in the middle of the paragraph.

81

Topic Sentences

Read the following paragraphs. Decide what would make a good topic sentence for each paragraph. Write it on the line above.

1. _____

The monkey shows are at 10:00 and 3:00 daily. The elephant show is performed on weekends at 2:00. The seals perform Monday, Wednesday, and Saturday at 11:00 and at 1:00 on the other days of the week. The shows will continue until the end of the summer.

2. _____

The Miller's children are Mike, age eight, Sandra, five years old, and b___ ___ months old. They have a dog, Blackie, and a cat, Tiger. The house ___ ___ ll.

3. _____

Hunters wear long underwear, be___ ___ ___ s and boots, and caps with earflaps. They h___ ___ out in the cold so long. Their vests and c___ ___ unters won't mistake them for a deer.

Sentences will vary.

4. _____

I could ___ ___ wind blew the rain against the window. The shutters beat against the hous___ ___ng, bang, bang. Lightning lit up the room. I was happy but tired when morning came. The storm had ended.

5. _____

Things were certainly different in New York than they were in Nebraska. Everyone seemed in such a hurry in New York. No one was very friendly in Emily's school. Emily and her brother, Ned, did not like their new community. They wished their dad would get transferred back to Nebraska.

6. _____

It opened Friday with folk dancing from around the world. All day Saturday and Sunday different countries exhibited their crafts and cooking. On Saturday night songs from all over the world were sung by the International Singers. There was a huge fireworks display at the festival's close Sunday night.

82

Topic Sentences

- Write a topic sentence for each of the following subjects. It should have enough content to be interesting and yet not reveal everything at once. "Answer" some of the "question" words and use descriptive words, too.

    Example: Frightened person: The frightened boy hid under the stairs.
    The frightened boy sat frozen in his hiding place under the stairs.
    Which one do you think is the better topic sentence?
    Why?

1. A special interest/hobby: _____

2. Eating at home: _____

3. A bee sting: _____

4. Myst___

5. Loud mu___

6. Cool clothes: _____

7. Uproarious laughter: _____

8. Least favorite thing: _____

Answers will vary.

83

Support Sentences

- Topic sentences often introduce a thought, subject, or event. They should be backed up by one or more **support sentences**.

    Example: The frightened boy sat frozen in his hiding place under the stairs. He watched as the prowler flashed his light around the room.

The second sentence, a support sentence, tells more about the first sentence.

Rewrite the eight topic sentences you wrote from the previous page. Write a support sentence for each one.

1. _____
2. _____
3. _____
4. _____
5. _____
6. _____
7. _____
8. _____

Sentences will vary.

84

Putting a Paragraph Together

Support sentences tell about the main idea expressed in the topic sentence. They support the topic sentence, and they support each other. Sentences that work together form a **paragraph**.

Read each topic sentence below. Write as many support sentences after it as it takes to answer the questions above each topic sentence. Write them in good order.

Questions: How do you know there are dogs available?
What kind are available?
What do you have to do to get one?

There are many dogs waiting to be adopted at the pound. _____

Questions: Why is he ___
W___

C___ six weeks. ___

Sentences will vary.

85

Writing a Paragraph

Choose a topic from the box. Write the topic of your choice on the line below.

_____

Write at least five facts about your topic.

_____
_____
_____
_____

| sister or brother |
| dogs as pets |
| after school responsibilities |
| the people next door |
| a mysterious package |

Look at what you have written. Do all ___ ___eas if you think they are important. Num___ ___ake sense. Write a topic sentence about t___ ___opic sentence with sentences that will sup___ ___bove help you write them.

Answers will vary.

Look at what you have written. Is there a topic sentence? Do the sentences following support it? Is there an order to them? Is what you have written interesting? Are your thoughts clearly stated? Rewrite what you have written so the answers to these questions will all be YES. Be sure and check your punctuation.

86

Writing Instructions in Sequence

This house painter wants to paint the trim on the roof. However, she has a little problem—she left out an important step. What is it?

She forgot to bring the bucket of paint with her when she climbed the ladder. In order to do anything—paint a house or brush your teeth—you have to perform a number of steps in the right **sequence**, or order.

Here is a list of steps for making papier-mâché. They are not in the correct sequence. Put them in the correct sequence on the lines below.

1. Dip the strips of newspaper into the mixture.

2. Apply the strips to the form.

3. Stir until the mixture is smooth, sticky, and wet.

4. Mix two parts water with one part flour.

First: _Mix two parts water with one part flour._

Next: _Stir until mixture is smooth, sticky, and wet._

Third: _Dip the strips of newspaper into the mixture._

Finally: _Apply the strips to the form._

87

Writing Instructions in Sequence

Write instructions for doing one of the following: blowing up a balloon; giving a dog a bath; making an ice-cream soda.

How to _____

First: _____

Next: _____

Third: _____

Finally: _____

Answers will vary.

Read the following instructions.

> **How Not to Paint the Floor**
>
> 1. Begin painting at the doorway and work your way into the room.
> 2. Paint around the furniture that is too heavy to move.
> 3. After painting one third of the room, sweep and wash the rest of the floor.
> 4. After you've painted yourself into a corner, walk across the floor and leave the room.

Now rewrite these instructions. Tell how one should really go about painting a floor. Use **sequence words** like *first, next, then,* and *last.* Sample answer given.

1. _First, move all the furniture out of the room._

2. _Next, sweep and wash the entire floor._

3. _Then, begin painting from one corner of the room, working your way towards the door._

4. _Finally, step outside the doorway and paint the remaining section near the door._

88

Writing a Direction Paragraph

A **paragraph** giving directions explains how to do something. Directions must be exact and in order.

Read the directions in the paragraph below and do what it tells you to do in the space to its right.

Draw a two inch square. Outside the upper left corner, write a **Q**. Outside the lower left corner, write an **F**. Outside the upper right corner, write a **D**. Outside the lower right corner, write a **T**. Draw a line from **D** to **F**. Draw a line from **T** to the **D-F** line. Make an **X** in the large triangle. Draw a face in the small triangle on the left. Color in the remaining triangle.

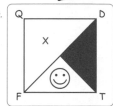

The directions above were given in an exact order. Sometimes directions use words that signal time like *first, next, now,* etc. Use the lines below to write a direction paragraph. Use words that signal time if you want. Give it to a friend to follow.

Answers will vary.

89

Writing a Descriptive Paragraph

A **descriptive paragraph** "paints" a picture in the reader's mind. Details help create a clearer picture.

After each of the following topic sentences, write details about what the sentences after them should describe.

The summer sun beat down on the big city's streets.

_____

The overturned flower vase on the desk was the first sign that the office was a mess.

_____

The old woman's face was parched from her ~~...~~

_____

The dachshund and the ~~...~~ ~~...~~king down the street together.

Choose o~~...~~ ~~...~~ntences from above. Rewrite it on the line below at the beginning ~~...~~ ~~...~~ragraph. Write three or four sentences after it that will describe what you s~~...~~d they should. Let detail words and phrases help create a strong descriptive paragraph.

Answers will vary.

90

Writing a Narrative Paragraph

A **narrative paragraph** tells about something that happened. The topic sentence should tell enough to make a reader want to read on. The sentences that follow the topic sentence are in the order in which they occurred.

After each of the following topic sentences, write a narrative paragraph using three or four sentences that show the order of events. Use your imagination to complete each paragraph.

On Sally's sixteenth birthday she got a car. _____

_____

A raccoon got into our garbage _____

Answers will vary.

Maggie crossed her fingers and shut her eyes when her father carried a large package into the house. _____

_____

91

Writing an Opinion Paragraph

The topic sentence in a paragraph that expresses an opinion tells what the writer thinks or feels. The other sentences in the paragraph state the reasons for the writer's opinion.

Written at the start of each paragraph below is a topic sentence expressing an opinion. Pretend, if necessary, that you are in agreement with that opinion. Write three sentences after the topic sentence backing your belief.

Vegetables are good for everyone. _____

_____

Studying with music produces the best _____

Sentences will vary.

Living in Antarctica would not be a lot of fun. _____

_____

92

Paragraph Building

Study this example to learn how to write a paragraph by answering the questions <u>who</u>, <u>where</u>, <u>when</u>, <u>how</u>, <u>what happened</u> or <u>what was done</u>.

TOPIC: A Class Trip

WHO: Mr. Thompson's and Miss Wilson's fourth grade classes went on a field

WHERE: trip. They went to a huge industrial bakery on Lovett Street in Tylerville.

WHEN: They left on Thursday morning at nine o'clock.

HOW: Some students rode in cars but most of the class rode on the school bus.

WHAT HAPPENED: When the group arrived at the bakery they were greeted by their tour guides and shown each step used in baking bread. At the end of the tour each child received a small loaf of bread to take home.

Write a paragraph about a class trip or family trip of your own. Answer these questions: who, where, when, how, what happened or what was done.

Answers will vary.

93

Expanding Paragraphs

Rewrite the paragraphs below. Combine some of the sentences. Add adjectives. Change some of the verbs and nouns and add details to make them more specific. Change the order of words and sentences. Make the paragraphs more interesting.

The children walk home after school. They walk past the candy shop. They like candy. They want to buy candy. They go in and look around. They pool their money. They buy one candy bar. They cut it in six pieces. They eat it on their walk home.

_____

Rex is my dog. He is a big dog. He is black and brown. He has black eyes. He has long ears. He likes to play. He does _____ friend.

Paragraphs will vary.

My sister is a pest. She comes in my room. She takes my things. She follows me. She wants to do what I do. She tells Mother on me. She cries.

_____

94

Expanding Paragraphs

Rewrite the paragraphs below. Use the material in each paragraph to create a better mental picture. Add details that will "paint" a mood or feeling and that will affect a reader's senses.

On summer nights my family sits on the porch after dinner. The fan blows air. My mom sometimes reads to us. Sometimes we talk or sing songs. Other times no one says a thing. We listen to the night. Summer nights with the family are nice.

Paragraphs will vary.

I smelled something _____ ____ ___ ___ was cooking dinner. She had made my favorit ___ ____ _____ begin my homework. I could still smell Mom's ___ ____ ___ dinner I hurried to the table.

95

Writing More Than One Paragraph

A paragraph is made up of sentences working together. Sometimes it takes more than one paragraph to tell something. Then paragraphs work together to tell about the main idea. Such writings have three parts. A beginning paragraph introduces what the composition is about. The middle part, which may be several paragraphs, backs up the main idea expressed in the introductory paragraph. The ending paragraph ties everything together. All of the paragraphs begin with topic sentences.

The main idea (**A**), the support, or middle, paragraphs (**B-D**), and the wrap-up (**E**) for **A Fourth of July Celebration** are written below. On a separate sheet of paper, jot down details you think might belong in each section. The details should answer the who, what, where, when, why, and how questions. Write at least three details.

A. The community was getting ready for the Fourth of July parade and picnic.

1. _____
2. _____
3. _____

D. The firemen got the fireworks display ready to go.

1. _____
2. _____
3. _____

B. All the cars and bikes looked like American flags.

1. _____
2. _____
3. _____

E. Th _____ eryone to ____ me stand

Answers will vary.

2. _____
3. _____

C. The L _____ to make the foo _____

1. _____
2. _____
3. _____

96

Using Notes in Writing Paragraphs

Write three paragraphs about what happens in the morning as you get ready for school. First make notes under the three topics listed below. Then write your paragraphs using your notes.

1. Who   2. What you do   3. What happens

Answers will vary.

97

Using Notes in Writing Paragraphs

A paragraph should be about one topic. First make brief notes about <u>bicycles</u> under the three topics listed below. Then write your paragraphs.

1. Description   2. Good points   3. Bad points

My bicycle is _____

One g _____

Answers will vary.

Another _____

Some bad points about a bicycle _____

98

Using Notes in Writing Paragraphs

One way to develop a paragraph is by using details. In order to do this an author must know about the topic.

In the exercises below, use encyclopedias, other reference books, and the Internet. First list details about the main idea as expressed in each topic sentence below. On another sheet of paper, rewrite each topic sentence as the first sentence in the paragraph. Follow it with three or four sentences that present details about the main idea expressed in the topic sentence.

The five Great Lakes are connected to each other by rivers or straits.

Details

_____

_____

Paragraph

Answers will vary.

Several _____ ...nce.
Details

_____

_____

Paragraph

_____

_____

_____

99

Combining Sentences

- A **compound sentence** is a sentence with two or more parts that are connected with a conjunction. Sentences that tell about the same person, place, or thing are easy to put together. When two words receive the same action of the verb, they can be combined into a compound object.
  Stacey likes math. Stacey likes art.
  Stacey likes **math and art**.

- A compound subject is two or more subjects that share a verb.
  Jill likes computers. Bob likes computers.
  Jill and Bob like computers.

If the subject that goes with the verb changes, be sure to check the verb form. In the first example above, the verb does not need to change. The subject is still just Stacey. In the second example, the subject is plural, so the verb must change. Verbs that go with plural subjects do not end in *s*.

- If you create a sentence with **I** and another person, do not forget that **I** always goes last.
  I like music. Megan likes music.
  Megan and I like music.

Practice

Combine each pair of sentences into one compound sentence.

1. I like dogs. My dad likes dogs.
   My dad and I like dogs.

2. My dad wants a beagle. I want a beagle.
   My dad and I want a beagle.

3. Pets need food. Pets need exercise.
   Pets need food and exercise.

100

Combining Sentences

A **compound verb** has two or more verbs that share the same subject and are joined by a conjunction.

- Some sentences tell about someone or something doing different things. These sentences are easy to combine. Sometimes you can combine them with **and**.
  I went to the library. I checked out some books.
  I went to the library **and** checked out some books.

- Sometimes it makes more sense to combine the sentences with **but**.
  I wanted a mystery. I couldn't find one.
  I wanted a mystery **but** couldn't find one.

Practice

Combine each pair of sentences into one compound sentence.

1. Bats eat insects. Bats pollinate plants.
   Bats eat insects and pollinate plants.

2. Bats hunt at night. Bats hide during the day.
   Bats hunt at night and hide during the day.

3. Bats stay cooler at night. Bats don't worry about predators at night.
   Bats stay cooler and don't worry about predators at night.

4. Some people are not afraid of bats. Some people put bat houses in their yards.
   Some people are not afraid of bats and put bat houses in their yards.

5. I will learn more about bats. I will know how to protect them.
   I will learn more about bats and will know how to protect them.

101

Combining Sentences

- This is a basic sentence.
  The horse jumped.

- Often readers would like more information. They might wonder where the horse jumped or what it looked like. Here is some more information about the horse.
  The horse jumped. The horse was gray.
  It went over the fence.

- All of this information can be combined into one sentence.
  The gray horse jumped over the fence.

- Sometimes, when you combine sentences, you can get rid of details that are obvious. Here, there is no need to say the rider was on the horse.
  A rider was on the horse. She was skillful. She held on to the reins.
  The skillful rider held on to the reins.

There will usually be more than one way to combine sentences. Just make sure the sentence makes sense.

Practice

Combine each pair of sentences into one compound sentence.

1. The robin was red. The robin made a nest. It was in a tree.
   The red robin made a nest in a tree.

2. The robin laid eggs. There were three. They were in the nest.
   The robin laid three eggs in the nest.

3. Our cat was curious. He tried to climb up the big tree. The tree was in our yard.
   Our curious cat tried to climb up the big tree in our yard.

102

Combining Sentences

Continue to practice combining the sentences below.

1. My dad cut down the tree. My dad chopped it into logs.
   My dad cut down the tree and chopped it into logs.

2. The class washed cars on Saturday to raise money.
   The class waxed cars on Saturday to raise money.
   The class washed and waxed cars on Saturday to raise money.

3. Mom bought three chances for a dollar. Mom won one of the prizes.
   Mom bought three chances for a dollar and won one of the prizes.

4. The dog jumped on my bed. The dog woke me.
   The dog jumped on my bed and woke me.

5. The girl scouts collect old papers. The boy scouts collect old papers.
   The girl scouts and boy scouts collect old papers.

6. Sarah prepared the potato salad. Sarah took it on the picnic.
   Sarah prepared the potato salad and took it on the picnic.

7. We bought a sailboat. We sailed it on Saturday.
   We bought a sailboat and sailed it on Saturday.

8. They nominated three candidates. They elected one of them class president.
   They nominated three candidates and elected one of them class president.

9. They visited their cousins. They visited their grandparents.
   They visisted their cousins and grandparents.

10. We went to the movie. We bought popcorn and candy during the intermission.
    We went to the movie and bought popcorn and candy during the intermission.

107

Combining Sentences

* Some sentences include just one simple idea.
  I wanted some extra money. My mom said I couldn't have any more allowance.
  I decided to start a pet-care business. I asked my friend to be my partner.

To improve your writing, look for ways to combine sentences to make your writing smoother.

* The sentences below probably do not sound right when they are read aloud.
  I wanted some extra money, my mom said I couldn't have any more allowance.
  I decided to start a pet-care business, I asked my friend to be my partner.

* To connect two sentences, you need more than just a comma. One way to connect them is to use words like *and, or, but,* or *so.*
  I wanted some extra money, **but** my mom said I couldn't have any more allowance.
  I decided to start a pet-care business, **so** I asked my friend to be my partner.

There is usually more than one way to combine sentences correctly.

Practice

Use commas and **and** or **but** to combine each pair of sentences below.

1. My mom really wanted me to take piano lessons. I didn't want to.
   My mom really wanted me to take piano lessons, but I didn't want to.

2. We decided I would take them for three months. Then we would talk about it again.
   We decided I would take them for three months, and then we would talk about it again.

3. I hate to admit it. I really like playing the piano.
   I hate to admit it, but I really like playing the piano.

108

Combining Sentences

Change the two sentences to one sentence by using the word given.
The first one is done for you.

1. It snowed. I could use my new snowshoes.   Suggested answers given.
   (because) I could use my snowshoes because it snowed.

2. We can play the game. The weather must be warm enough.
   (but) We can play the game but the weather must be warm enough.

3. The magician performed. The audience was spellbound.
   (when) The audience was spellbound when the magician performed.

4. The children washed the windows. The grocer gave them money.
   (so) The children washed the windows, so the grocer gave them money.

5. Lois played the piano. Her brother played a flute solo.
   (while) Lois played the piano while her brother played a flute solo.

6. We jumped into the canoe. There were no paddles.
   (but) We jumped into the canoe but there were no paddles.

7. Finish your lunch. Please clean your room.
   (after) Please clean your room after you finish your lunch.

8. We went to the ball game. We ate lunch.
   (before) We ate lunch before we went to the ballgame.

9. She returned the sweater. It didn't fit.
   (since) She returned the sweater since it didn't fit.

109

Combining Sentences

Sometimes several sentences can be combined. One sentence contains the main thought and each of the others adds only a word or two to the main sentence.

Combine the sentences in each group into one sentence.
Add only the important words to the main sentence.
The first one is done for you.

1. The dog ran down the street. The dog was barking. The street was crowded.
   The barking dog ran down the crowded street.

2. The snake went through the grass. The grass was tall. The snake was fast.
   The fast snake went through the tall grass.

3. The girls baked a cake. It was a chocolate cake. There were three girls.
   The three girls baked a chocolate cake.

4. John finished the race. The race was two miles. He was first.
   John finished the two mile race first.

5. The boy brought his bike inside. His bike was damaged. The boy was unhappy.
   The unhappy boy brought his damaged bike inside.

6. Sara ate the treat. The treat was ice cream. She ate it quickly.
   Sara quickly ate the ice cream treat.

7. The birds sang songs. The birds were red. The songs were pretty.
   The red birds sang pretty songs.

8. Trees grow in the forest. They are elm trees. The forest is cool.
   Elm trees grow in the cool forest.

110

Combining Sentences

- Some sentences look almost exactly the same.
  I wanted yogurt. I wanted a muffin. I wanted cereal.

- Reading several similar sentences in a row like these can be boring. Try combining them into a series. If you name more than two things, put a comma after each one except the last one. Put **and** before the last one. Follow this rule even if you have more than three things.
  I wanted yogurt, a muffin, **and** cereal.

- Here is another example:
  I was tired. I was hungry. I was thirsty. I was grumpy.
  I was tired, hungry, thirsty, **and** grumpy.

- If you have just two items, you need **and**, but you do not need any commas.
  I wanted milk. I wanted orange juice.
  I wanted milk **and** orange juice.

Practice

Combine the groups of sentences into one sentence.

1. I invited Mario. I invited Ken. I invited Lee.
   I invited Mario, Ken, and Lee.

2. We went skating. We played video games. We ate pizza.
   We went skating, played video games, and ate pizza.

3. We talked about school. We talked about baseball. We talked about this summer.
   We talked about school, baseball, and this summer.

4. We helped Dad wash the dishes. We helped Dad clean the family room.
   We helped Dad wash the dishes and clean the family room.

103

Combining Sentences

- Some sentences can be combined using words such as *after, as, because, before, if, when,* and *while.*
  I was feeling ill. I went home from school early.
  I went home from school early **because** I was feeling ill.

A **clause** is a group of words that has a subject and a verb. In the sentence above, *I went home from school early* is a **main clause**. It can stand alone. *Because I was feeling ill* is a **dependent clause**. It cannot stand alone. Words like *because, when, after,* and *until* are used to introduce a dependent clause.

- Watch the order of the sentences you are combining. How you arrange them will affect their meaning. The following sentence has the same words as the sentence above, but it does not really mean the same thing.
  I was feeling ill **because** I went home from school early.

- If the dependent clause comes before the main clause, put a comma after the dependent clause.
  When I still felt ill the next day, I went to the doctor.

Practice

Combine each pair of sentences to make one sentence. Use the connecting words **because, when, after,** and **until.** Be sure to put the sentences together in an order that makes sense.

1. I opened the mailbox and saw a butterfly. I was surprised.
   I was surprised when I opened the mailbox and saw a butterfly.

2. I forgot to get the mail out. I was watching the butterfly.
   I forgot to get the mail out because I was watching the butterfly.

3. I watched the butterfly. It flew away.
   I watched the butterfly until it flew away.

4. It happened yesterday. I wrote about it in my journal.
   I wrote about it in my journal after it happened yesterday.

104

Combining Sentences

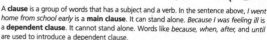

- One way to make sure the reader understands how two sentences are related is to combine them using a dependent clause.
  Mark uses a wheelchair. No one expected him to play basketball.
  Because Mark uses a wheelchair, no one expected him to play basketball.

A **clause** is a group of words that has a subject and a verb. In the sentence above, *no one expected him to play basketball* is a **main clause** that can stand alone. *Because Mark uses a wheelchair* is a **dependent clause** that cannot stand alone.

- Words like *although, because, if, since, before, after, when,* and *even though* are used to introduce dependent clauses. Look at these examples. Notice that the two parts of the combined sentence are separated by a comma.
  When Mark challenged Rick to a game, Rick wasn't sure what to say.
  Because Mark was his friend, he said yes.

Practice

Rewrite each pair of sentences as one sentence. Start with the word in parentheses.

1. She is not the fastest runner. She is the most popular team member. (Although)
   Although she is not the fastest runner, she is the most popular team member.

2. She supports her teammates. She is fun to have at track meets. (Because)
   Because she supports her teammates, she is fun to have at track meets.

3. She loses a race. She shakes the winner's hand. (After)
   After she loses a race, she shakes the winner's hand.

4. She has such a positive attitude. She deserves a blue ribbon! (Because)
   Because she has such a positive attitude, she deserves a blue ribbon!

105

Combining Sentences

Practice combining the sentences below.

1. Harry climbed the oak tree.
   Nate climbed the oak tree.
   Harry and Nate climbed the oak tree.

2. The fifth grade played the teachers in soccer.
   The sixth grade played the teachers in soccer.
   The fifth and sixth grades played the teachers in soccer.

3. Cory cut strips of paper to make chains.
   Cory pasted strips of paper to make chains.
   Cory cut and pasted strips of paper to make chains.

4. We saw the lion show at the zoo.
   We saw the monkey show at the zoo.
   We saw the lion and the monkey shows at the zoo.

5. Mother bought a lot of food for the family party.
   Mother cooked a lot of food for the family party.
   Mother bought and cooked a lot of food for the family party.

6. The children shivered when they got out of the cold water.
   The children shook when they got out of the cold water.
   The children shivered and shook when they got out of the cold water.

7. The scouts will sell lemonade to raise money.
   The scouts will sell cookies to raise money.
   The scouts will sell lemonade and cookies to raise money.

8. Our class studied about famous Americans.
   Our class wrote about famous Americans.
   Our class studied and wrote about famous Americans.

106

Friendly and Business Letters
Capitalization

- The street, city, state, and month are always capitalized in the heading.
  1415 **H**igh **S**treet
  Hometown, **VT** 02345
  March 8, 1998

- If you are writing a business letter, be sure to capitalize the person's title and name; the company's name if you include it; the names of the street and city, and state abbreviations. (Note: A list of state abbreviations appears on pg. 128.)
  Ms. **E**lizabeth **S**cott
  River **C**ity **P**ublishers
  4410 **M**ain Street
  Greensville, **TX** 77701

- The greeting and the name are capitalized, as well as the first word of the closing.
  Dear Elizabeth,   **D**ear **M**s. Wilkins,   **S**incerely yours,

Practice

Read the friendly letter. Circle five words that should be capitalized.

> 210 Avondale (street)
> Elmview, (ny) 08780
> (june) 6, 2001
>
> (dear) Fred,
>
> I am a big fan of mystery books. Thanks for sending the books to me on my birthday. What would you like for your birthday?
>
> (your) fan,
> Esther Martinez

111

Friendly Letters
Punctuation

A friendly letter is a letter you write to someone you know well, like a friend or relative. It might be a thank-you note or just friendly news.

- A heading with a return address and the date is put in the upper right corner of your letter. That way, your reader will have your address and will know when you wrote your letter. Place a comma between the city and state abbreviations and between the date and the year.
  Bowling Green, OH   June 7, 2001

- The letter begins with the greeting and the name. Put a comma after the name.
  Dear Elise,

  Next comes the body of the letter. This is whatever you want to say. When you are finished, you need a closing. Put a comma after the closing.
  Your friend,

Practice

Add four commas where they are needed in the letter below.

> 735 Brookhaven Drive
> Antioch, TN 77013
> January 17, 2000
>
> Dear Aunt Mollie,
>
> Thank you for sending me a T-shirt for my birthday. I'll wear it a lot. I hope you can come visit us soon. Maybe you can come to one of my violin recitals.
>
> Love,
> Amber

112

Business Letters
Punctuation

A business letter is a formal letter you write to a company or to a person you do not know very well. The form and rules of punctuation used are different than those used when writing a friendly letter.

A comma goes after the date and city names in the heading and the inside address. A period goes after an abbreviation such as Mr. in the inside address and the greeting. The greeting is followed by a colon. Words and phrases such as Yours truly, Sincerely, or Best regards in the closing are followed by a comma.

> 999 Ninth Avenue
> Lakeside, ID 85567   — **Heading**
> June 7, 2000
>
> Mr. Victor Costa
> Channel 7 News
> 777 Seven Street   — **Inside Address**
> Lakeside, ID 84224
>
> Dear Mr. Costa: ←——— **Greeting**
>
>   Yours truly, ←——— **Closing**
>   *Jenna Linkwood* ←——— **Signature**
>   Jenna Linkwood

Practice

Add the correct punctuation to the heading, the inside address, and the greeting.

1. **Heading:**
   Foxwood Elementary School
   3498 Washington Street
   Creekville, KS 71115
   April 17, 2000

2. **Inside Address:**
   Ms. Yolanda Moore
   Moore Bakery
   1212 Main Street
   Creekville, KS 11115

3. **Greeting:**
   Dear Ms. Moore,

113

Writing a Friendly Letter

Write a letter to a friend, thanking him or her for a gift you received on your birthday. Be sure to use good letter form and correct capitalization and punctuation.

Answers will vary.

114

Proofreading Practice:
Friendly Letter

Follow the directions below to show each part of a friendly letter.

Circle the:

Heading—orange   Greeting—green   Body—blue
Closing—yellow   Signature—purple

As you read the letter below, you will notice there are errors in capitalization and punctuation. Read the letter carefully. Use the proofreader's marks that you have learned to correct capitalization and insert commas where they are needed.

201 pioneer road
trenton nj 21570
june 5, 2001

dear ken griffey, jr.

You are my favorite baseball player. I admire your high batting average and get excited every time you hit a homerun. I'm sorry you were hurt during the '96 season and couldn't play for awhile.

My grandpa saw you play when you were just a little kid. It was at a father-son game when your dad ken griffey sr. played for the cincinnati reds. Grandpa said you looked like a natural athlete even then.

I am sending along one of your baseball cards. Could you please autograph it and send it back to me? I would really appreciate it.

your fan

richard e. anderson

115

Writing a Business Letter

Write a letter in response to the ad on the right. Tell why you are writing the letter. Tell about yourself and why you would be a good candidate for the job. Be sure to use good letter form and correct capitalization and punctuation.

Part-time summer work for student. Train on Job. Assist in Bike Shop. References. Write Joe Bickle, Box 56, Craig, CO 81625

Heading   your street address
           your city, state and zip
           date

Inside Address
Mr. Joe Bickle
Box 56
Craig, CO 81625

Greeting
Dear Mr. Bickle   :

Body
Letters will vary.

Closing   your name   ,
Signature

116

Proofreading Practice:
Business Letter

Follow the directions below to show each part of a business letter.
Circle the:

heading—purple   inside address—red   greeting—blue
body—green   closing—orange   signature—yellow

201 Valleyview Road
Phoenix, AZ 37715
August 24, 2001

Mr. Fix R. Upp, CEO
Lemon Motors Corp.
1000 Motorway Avenue
Detroit, MI 64718

Dear Mr. Fix R. Upp:

I bought my 2001 Super Duper sports car in March of 2001 and have noticed several problems. Whenever I turn my parking lights on, the horn honks until I turn them off. My right turn signal makes the right window go down. Whenever I step on the brakes my radio blares full blast. I have never been able to get the car's trunk to open. I realize these are minor problems but they are driving me crazy! Please do something promptly.

Respectfully,
Mrs. Wanna Newcar

117

Addressing Envelopes:

Now that you have learned how to write a letter, you need to learn how to address an envelope. In the upper right corner of the envelope, write your name. Below your name, write your street address. The next line should include your city, state, and Zip code. In the center of the envelope, write the name of the person to whom you are writing. On the line below the person's name, write that person's street address followed by the person's city, state, and Zip code. Remember to capitalize the names of people and places. Also notice the comma placed between the city and state.

Dr. T. W. Smith
746 Lorain Lane
Chicago, IL 84417

Ms. Elizabeth Cornwell
P. O. Box 1945
770 Sunset Boulevard
Pasadena, CA 51012

Look at the envelope below. Correct the capitalization and punctuation. Use the envelope above to help you.

brad springer
500 juniper road
tampa fl 14158

brent g. collins
3414 arlington drive
denver, co 32717

118

NOTES

NOTES

NOTES

NOTES